Our Sacred Ocean

Is Suffering Now

Our Sacred Ocean - Is Suffering Now

VIC HUMMERT

ISBN-13: 978-1495990274
ISBN-10: 1495990273

Table of Contents

Foreword

Among multiplying books on Earth's human-caused and continuing loss of ecologic health, Victor Hummert's Our Sacred Ocean is an indispensable masterpiece, with abounding scientific data the author combines moving anecdotes from his experience as clergyman, world traveler and activist, prison chaplain, and skilled poet and storyteller.

While identifying global human-caused dangers to ocean well-being, essential to human and non-human animal health, and the author most often calls on his twenty-year experience in ocean-sided Louisiana and specifically New Orleans and Lafayette. In the context of global warming due to excessive fossil-fuel usage, he cites also technological trashing acidifying the ocean possibly beyond repair. Jellyfish he perceives as major contributors to ocean poisoning and extinction of fish indispensable to an adequate food supply for increasing billions of human as well as non-human consumers.

Such ocean deterioration, largely due to human callousness, must be halted immediately if major tragedies are to be averted. That is Victor Hummert's powerful message in his mind-stretching and soul-stirring book, Our Sacred Ocean.

Margaret Berry, PhD
Professor Emerita, John Carroll University

Our oceans, the place of our evolutionary birth, where our sustenance is bound, is suffering. Hummert's analysis is spot on, a wonderful commentary on the state of our synthetic seas. Reading this will give you a baseline understanding where we are in ocean conservation, and where we go from here.

Marcus Eriksen, PhD
Executive Director of the 5 Gyres Institute

Preface

Mary Heffron and Tom Fenton have patiently, generously proof read, then published several previous books of Environmental Haiku. Aware of my being "gainfully unemployed" many hours of tedious work were "free labor" from Mary and Tom.

Adam Chandler (**adam@vichummert.org**) has been my "tec" adviser since 1995. Adam is a librarian in Cornell University who generously posts thousands of haiku on the site he easily set up. Without several skilled friends, as expressed in previous books of haiku, not much would be accomplished. I am deeply grateful to all who have tutored me in publishing books that appeal for our care of Earth in peril. This latest effort is a special, singular appeal on the part of *Our Sacred Ocean* which is suffering silently.

Bob Chaney (**bob@vichummert.org**) of Lafayette, LA is a retired science teacher who was my first patient tutor in the world of computers. Bob Herring (**bob@davcommdigital.com**), also from Lafayette, LA is my latest godsend in technology. I am deeply grateful to all for technical help.

Not least, January 2014 brought the coldest weather in decades to the southern regions of the USA. A "state of emergency" was declared for Lafayette which allowed me to finish writing a few elementary thoughts about our ocean in rapid decline. Friends in Louisiana chide me over concern about climate change and global warming. My only response is to invite all to check the scene in Queensland, Australia where their summer brought brush fires and temperatures of 130 degrees Fahrenheit.

And as this book is being written and ready for publishing by my friends, I eagerly await Pope Francis' encyclical (letter to the world), tentatively entitled,

"The Ecology of Mankind,"
a phrase used by Pope Benedict to describe not only how people must defend and respect nature but how the nature of the person – masculine and feminine as created by God – must also be defended,"
according to Vatican Radio. (**CWN - January 27, 2014)**[1]

It should be released in 2014 and will certainly be a positive message to share with all the world concerning the environment.

I continue writing out of concern for future generations who must survive in a sweltering climate and will not enjoy birds or gifts of nature that were mine since childhood.

---

[1] http://www.catholicculture.org/news/headlines/index.cfm?storyid=20300

Without meadowlarks
Our lives are spiritually
Deprived forever

Forests of Illinois[2]
Were my sole paradise that
Disappeared quickly

Following the 2013 appearance *of Fourth Quarter Haiku,* I decided to just write occasional guest columns about Earth care for the Lafayette DAILY ADVERTISER. Lafayette, many know is called "Oil City". It is the "Hub City" for thousands of oil rigs in the Gulf. The "oil patch" is served by Petroleum Helicopters International (PHI), supposedly with the largest fleet of helicopters in the world. When hurricanes come, workers must be snatched from the oil rigs and brought back to shore safely. Drilling for oil continues daily in the Gulf of Mexico. Gulf coast politicians are beholden to energy corporations.

As Earth sends more powerful messages in the form of "weather events" globally, someone could keep reminding oil and gas CEO's that solar, wind, and other sources of energy must eventually replace fossil fuels. Mark Jacobson, a professor in Stanford University was invited by David Letterman one night to explain there is enough solar, wind, and other renewable energy sources to power the planet. Letterman was convinced and saw immediately where the resistance would be found.

How do we convince energy moguls of this fact when billions of dollars are at stake? Is oil a global addiction also?

Will we discover
Earth is demanding our shift
In energy sources?

---

[2] During my childhood in southern Illinois I was taught by Victor Joseph Hummert, an "ecologist" before the word existed. Affectionately known as "VJ", my father took me hunting and fishing. He had no idea I would stop hunting any creatures after shooting two beautiful mallard ducks on Frogtown Lake, near Breese, IL in 1955, then end up becoming a vegetarian in 1984. Grandfather Henry B. Hummert (biography is available on Google) began the Breese-Trenton coal mining company with three bituminous coal mines operating in Breese, during my childhood. No one in the family would have envisioned my total support for renewable energy and closing down fossil fuels. Please check out the website **www.fossilfree.org** for ways to protect Earth.

"DRILLING = JOBS"[3]
In Louisiana now
Becoming water[4]

If we do not change sources of energy eventually, children of today will be trapped in a future replete with catastrophic occurrences such as Katrina, (New Orleans – 2005) Irene (2011) and Sandy (2012), both hitting NYC and the Atlantic coast as wrath of nature. Disastrous storms are beginning to fade from Louisiana memories in 2014. The Weather Channel (October 29, 2013) estimated Katrina's damage to be $80 billion. On the anniversary of hurricane Sandy, Weather Channel reporters concluded 300,000 homes were damaged or destroyed in New Jersey and 300,000 were hit in New York City. NYC officials in 2013 have placed huge inflatable tubes in the subway system that will expand to prevent water from flooding the subway system.

Automatic floodgates elsewhere will pop up to prevent another storm from entering the subway entrances. However, there are vents on NYC streets that will allow water to enter. Saltwater coming into contact with the electric tracks will wreak much damage. Nature, as always, will have the last word. The latest "word" from nature arrived (November 2013) in the Philippines as super storm Haiyan wreaked devastation with the most powerful winds ever recorded.

Will we learn to live   *We must move threatened*
With fewer fossil fuels?   *Lighthouses[6] is sufficient proof*
Ocean demands so[5]   *Ocean is coming*

My choice of not writing any more small books was abruptly reconsidered in September 2013. Dr. Arthur Milholland, a faculty member in the University of Maryland School of Medicine sent a book review about jellyfish and the future of our ocean to me. From the review of the 2013 book entitled *Stung! On Jellyfish Blooms and the future of the Ocean,* I discovered more clearly how our collective oceanic future is now intertwined with jellyfish.

I phoned Jacoby Carter, PhD, a researcher of invasive species who works with the US Geological Survey (USGS) Wetlands Center in Lafayette. There isn't too much in the environmental area that Jacoby does not know about. It became apparent Jacoby and other friends in Louisiana were not aware

---

[3] Seen on doors of Lafayette business establishments and some of 460+ restaurants in the prosperous city. Those who question the petroleum economy are viewed as a "raspberry seeds in the cavities" of oil CEO's

[4] Every twenty minutes an area of Louisiana the size of a football field drifts into the Gulf of Mexico. Much of the soil/marsh coastal erosion is due to 50,000 miles of oil or gas pipelines traversing the state.

[5] Benjamin Strauss of Climate Central and Wendy Koch (USA TODAY, 29/July/2013) caution 300 to 1,400 US cities and towns might be submerged before 2100 if more storm surges enter their areas.

[6] Lighthouses from Maine to Miami and California had to be moved back from the Atlantic and Pacific coasts as the rising ocean encircles their foundations.

of this important book on the spread of jellyfish. I soon felt compelled to summarize the 400 page book by compiling a brief commentary on the subject. You, the honorable reader of this elementary book might be inclined to read Lisa-ann Gershwin's excellent but troubling volume. In trying to write another haiku book, a word of my personal concern would be expressed for our ocean in rapid decline. And you as exploring readers will perceive "jellies" are on the rise everywhere. May you never be stung by a jellyfish!

Vic Hummert, Lafayette, LA
February 2014

In memory of the Exxon Valdez, a cosmic suffering of Alaska, March 24, 1989.

Introduction

I've had the pleasure of meeting Vic shortly after returning to my native home of Lafayette, Louisiana, after doing my time in the military. Getting to know Vic has been a very inspiring time for me, and as God would have it, during a time of major growth in my own Spiritual Journey. I continually saw similarities between my weekend retreats I participated in and my Men's small groups I was a part of. The similarities revolved around finding God in Nature. I began to truly appreciate Nature as a gift from God. And as I listened to Vic, I became aware of just how much he believes that as well.

In June 2013, I purchased two copies of the book *Spiritual Ecology: The Cry of the Earth* and gave one to Vic. I stumbled upon the book through my incessant need to learn more and more about God and Nature as I read books by Richard Rohr, Bill Plotkin, and Belden C. Lane, and many others. A dear friend of Vic's, Thomas Berry, has a contributed story in *Spiritual Ecology* and Vic mentions that in one of his latest books. Another book that Vic and I share an affinity toward, is the book, "Stung!" that he writes about later in this book. There are many organizations that tell of the plight of the dying seas. It isn't being spoken of enough.

As my knowledge grew, from my readings, my men's groups, and spending time with Vic, so too did my appreciation for preserving what precious resources we have left. Vic's haiku have been a wonderful medium to become aware and open-minded to enacting change and spreading the message. It is my belief that we as human beings exploit the Earth in pursuit of a "better way of life. "

As St. Francis heard God's call to "restore My Church on Earth," so too is God's message the same for us now. The Church is God's people, and that isn't just humankind. It's also all things created, and many, many people have taken advantage of nature and subsequently abused the Earth.

Vic's stories and haiku, remind us to appreciate and honor all things of this Earth. I believe Vic's message is clear and we all benefit from awakening our soul to what is around us. We cannot be fully awake and ignore the gifts God provides at the same time.

Vic is an example of great stewardship and authentic compassion for those that can't speak for themselves.

Bob Herring, Lafayette, LA
Content Strategist, DavcommDigital, LLC
February 2014

Chapter 1 - One Sting Remains Forever

When I finally received Gershwin's book from the Lafayette library I immediately recalled my 1971 dive from a small yacht into the South China Sea a short distance from Clearwater Bay, Kowloon, Hong Kong. Jack Cuff, a Maryknoll priest friend from Chicago stood on the deck some twenty feet above calm, relatively clear water. From his vantage point Jack saw jellyfish encircling me and called out a warning. I knew it would be risky to push them aside. I felt somewhat safer as he took a long pole from the boat and told me he would use it to drive the jelly fish away. In his first attempt to protect me, a jellyfish was hoisted above the water.

The amorphous creature, nearly two feet in length, was hanging from the pole. As the boneless jellyfish was being lifted away, it broke into several pieces. Numerous scattered tentacles were then carried by a small wave on to my shoulders and chest. I froze with pain as all parts of the fragmented jelly, in the process of falling apart, continued clinging to, and biting me. Going into a survival mode with the jelly stinging away, my attention shifted to staying afloat since no one was near to pry the disintegrating jelly from me, or holds my head above South China Sea water. Doubtless, other swimmers would not want to challenge such hostile creatures. Struggling to avoid drowning I simply allowed the dismembered jelly to continue pelting me with painful bites for too long. The jelly assault lasted at least five minutes. I was in my durable thirties at the time.

The rude introduction to jellyfish in Hong Kong waters remains a very unpleasant memory forty years later. I know instantly when reading of encounters why beaches in tourist areas would be closed by jellies.

Stung! by Lisa-ann Gershwin is such a powerful well-documented study that I felt a need to write one more small volume beyond *Fourth Quarter Haiku*. I am simply trying to summarize an important 400-page book for anyone who might be too busy to follow how our ocean is slowly dying – while jellyfish thrive. Gershwin's book was published by the University of Chicago Press.

Paul Dayton of the Scripps Institution of Oceanography wrote this blurb on the cover: "Read this book! You know that the oceans are in trouble, but this is the most comprehensive and clear explanation of why. Stung! Is more than just a book about jellyfish, it is undoubtedly one of the best books detailing the stresses on our ocean ecosystems. It is a much needed and spectacular achievement."

Author of *The Ocean of Life* and Professor of Ocean Conservation Callum Roberts from the University of York, England adds: "Stung! is an enthusiastic guide to the extraordinary story of jellyfish, a group that dominated the world's oceans of half a billion years ago, and in the present form, may come to do so again if we don't curb the rising tide of human damage to the sea."

Sylvia Earle, founder of the Sylvia Earle Alliance and Mission Blue (www.mission-blue.org), added a cosmic dimension in writing: "By picking jellyfish and telling their stories, Lisa-ann Gershwin masterfully shows how they and we are hitched together – and everything else in the universe."

We instinctively recall how graphic photos of parched soil in times of drought might drive us to think of Earth's future without food. (Please read "Who Will Feed the World?" THE CHRISTIAN SCIENCE MONITOR – 9/24/2012)

"NO FARMS NO FOOD" is a logo of the American Farmland Trust (**www.farmland.org**)

During the Cold War, KGB agents in the USA called for an immediate end to the arms race. Soviet spies concluded US farmland was succumbing to roads and "development" so fast that the USA would not be able to feed its own people within 100 years. The mighty USA would eventually become an importer of food despite all of the available land. There are 3.79 million square miles in the USA.

Our ocean was once considered by food scientists as a major source of nourishment. Is more media attention now devoted to sporting events than to the slow, steady loss of farmland and our increasingly acidic ocean?

Burning fossil fuels since the 1700's is on the increase. In 1914, the year of Thomas Berry's birth, the ecological prophet remarked, "There were only one million cars." In 2014 there are 300 million vehicles in the US. Each gallon of gasoline emits twenty-two pounds of carbon dioxide. Simply imagine twenty-two balloons emerging from tail pipes as we travel our roads. Each second well over 10,000 gallons of gasoline go up into the atmosphere, that will remain for hundreds of years.

One gallon becomes　　　　　　　　*How do we prevent*
Twenty-two choking pounds of　　*Millions of vehicles[7] from*
Carbon dioxide　　　　　　　　　*Destroying our lives?*

US cars and factories spewed out 5.8 billion tons of carbon dioxide in 2012, down 3.8 percent. If we transition to electric cars that are charged from a grid burning fossil fuels, what possible gain is made? We might obtain electricity from solar panels, then recharge electric cars directly from a renewable source.

Both Mr.& Mrs. Joseph Weisbrich, immigrants from Germany, worked for Governor Nelson Rockefeller in Pocantico Hills, NY since the 1960's. After years of faithful service they were invited to live in nicer quarters above Rockefeller's garage filled with a collection of cars. Before leaving for Hong Kong in 1970 I visited the Weisbrich family. Tight security and escorts brought us into the garage passing through a large collection of cars. I could not count them, but did see an electric car from 1913. Does the Rockefeller collection outnumber Jay Leno's 100 cars and 80 motorcycles?

Henry Bliss was the first pedestrian to be killed by an electric taxi on September 13, 1899 as he tried to assist a woman step down from a trolley on 74th & Central Park in New York City. Bliss is the first recorded fatality from vehicles. Since 1899 over thirty million have died in car accidents, three million in the 20th century alone. Nearly 30,000 persons are killed in US car accidents each year. A similar number of US citizens die from gun violence yearly. What is the most deadly consumer item – cars or guns?

---

[7] 3/4 of Los Angeles and ½ of every major city in the US are set aside for roads, parking garages or business firms linked to buying, selling and maintaining private cars. Cities with over 100,000 people are gridlocked at least twice daily. Lafayette, LA at noon is "stressed" from drivers who opt to have lunch far from their place of work. Bikers are at risk in Lafayette.

If we had declared cars as our "enemy" would humans not have surrendered long ago? Since such a declaration about private cars isn't likely to be made, we will continue losing one person in car accidents every fifteen minutes. Insurance agents testify everyone at some point in life is involved in a car accident.

Unsafe at Any Speed by Ralph Nader (1965) applies to more than one model of private cars. *Autogeddon* written by Heathcoate Williams in 1994 is a companion indictment of automobiles.

In 2000 there were 3,936,229 miles of roads in the US. By 2009 there were 6.1 million miles of roads. In 2014 there were more than 8 million miles of roads in the nation. Our European ancestors carried out the "largest land grab ever," according to historians. Limitless burning of fossil fuels means billions of tons of carbon dioxide emissions are turning our ocean into carbonic acid. From high school chemistry we learned carbon dioxide coming into contact with water becomes mild carbonic acid (H_2CO_3). Our ocean is changing constantly, to the detriment of all life on Earth. Jellyfish are thriving while other forms of marine life fade away.

Would we allow soil
To be lost as our ocean
Now declines in health?

Earth's warming ocean
Serves as incubator for
Harmful jellyfish

Jellyfish might be
Biblical locust plagues for
Uncaring humans

Jellyfish alone
Can stop navy ships without
Launching of missiles[8]

Jellies can shut down ships, passively cripple nuclear and/ or ordinary power plants, end desalination operations and quickly close tourist beaches. Some swimmers have died from encounters with jellies.

Apart from ocean sunfish and turtles now declining in numbers, jellies have few known predators. There are different jelly fish species, some of which will attack other species. Gershwin reports, "Jellyfish are voracious feeders. Mnemiopsis jellyfish (pronounced "me-knee-op-sis") is able to eat over ten times its own body weight in food, and to double in size, each day. They can do this because they are metabolically speaking, tremendously efficient, being able to put more of the energy they ingest toward growth than more complex creatures they compete with. And they can be wasteful. Mnemiopsis act like a fox in the henhouse. After they gorge themselves, they continue to collect and kill prey. As far as the

---

[8] "On July 27,2006 the USS Ronald Reagan, then the most modern aircraft carrier in existence was docked in the port of Brisbane, Australia. New Zealand is a foe of nuclear power/weapons. The Nuclear Free Zone treaty bans any nuclear vessel from entering New Zealand's ports. Australia was the logical choice for the USS Reagan to dock. The commander of US Naval Air Forces announced "an acute case of fouling" had forced the vessel to remain in port. Thousands of jellyfish had been sucked into the ship's nuclear power cooling system. Australia's newspapers ran the headline – "Jellyfish take on US warship."(THE NEW YORK REVIEW OF BOOKS, September 26, 2013)

ecosystem goes, the result is the same whether the jellyfish digest the food or not: they go on killing until nothing is left. That can happen quickly.

One study showed that mnemiopsis removed over 30 percent of the copepod (small marine crustaceans) population to it each day…Jellyfish can eat anything, and often do." Some don't even need to eat, in the usual sense of the word. They simply absorb dissolved organic matter through their epidermis. Others have algae living in their cells that provide food through photosynthesis (processing energy directly from the sun)…The question of jellyfish death is vexing. If jellyfish fall on hard times, they can simply 'de – grow'. That is, they reduce in size, but their bodies remain in proportion. That's a very different outcome from what is seen in starving fish, or people. And when food becomes available again, jellyfish simply recommence growing. Some individual jellyfish live for a decade. But the polyp survives pretty much indefinitely by cloning. One polyp colony started in 1935 and is still alive and well in a laboratory in Virginia."

As I perused her book, it was necessary to pause, check footnotes, then read again Gershwin's study of jellies. It flowed like a science fiction horror story. At this point, you, the reader may have contacted your local library for a copy of one landmark book on our ocean in decline. Or bought it for marking special pages. The book is stunning, frightening too.

"Where humans add nutrients to water (such as fertilizer runoff from farms), areas with depleted oxygen, known as eutrophied zones, form. They can occur naturally, but are spreading quickly as oceans become filled with excess phosphorus and nitrogen derived from a variety of agriculture and industrial human activities. In river estuaries, and in confined waters such as the Baltic, the Black Sea, and the Gulf of Mexico, eutrophied zones have spread to a frightening extent, and they appear to be permanent. Nothing that needs even moderate amounts of oxygen, including fish, shellfish, prawns, and crabs, can survive in them. But the jellyfish survive."

Living in Lafayette, the "dead zone" appears in our media often. How big is it really? The dead zone in the Gulf of Mexico in 2013 was the size of Connecticut. (5,543 sq. miles) Louisiana is 52, 843 square miles. TransCanada and other promoters of the Keystone XL (KXL) pipeline bringing tar sands oil to Louisiana are presently devastating over 50,000 square miles of pristine forest land in Alberta, Canada.

Their goal is to transport oil to Texas for processing. Tar sands oil is three times more harmful to the planet than ordinary crude oil. Our sacred ocean will also suffer more under the influence of KXL's bitumen effluent. The final decision rests with Obama and the US State Department. Portions of KXL have already been assembled from Alberta to Cushing, Oklahoma.

An executive order by Mr. Obama could halt the plunge into greater environmental problems for Earth. Our ocean is already becoming too acidic from fossil fuel burning. KXL was not mentioned in Obama's January address to the nation. Is he fidgeting, fearful of oil magnates?

Failing to perceive
Acidity closing in
How will we survive[9]?

To the question – "How and what do jellyfish eat?" Gershwin provides some insights that again brought me back to the personal jellyfish encounter while swimming in Hong Kong waters. For a few unpleasant moments was I becoming lunch for a dying jellyfish?

"Most jellyfish eat by capturing prey on their tentacles. Cnidarian jellyfish use their stinging cells for that purpose, essentially stunning or killing their prey with venom and a harpoon injury. Ctenophores ensnare their prey with sticky threads. Trying to brush the tentacles off my shoulders just widened the zone of attack over my body. My hand was stung most often for trying to push off pieces of the disintegrating jellyfish. A science teacher in Lafayette explained that jellyfish shoot little harpoons into anything they attack.

Two women in 2013 attempted the 100-mile swim from Cuba to Florida. June 12, 2013, Australian endurance swimmer Chloe McCardel ended her swim because of jellyfish stings.

Diana Nyad, 64 was successful in her long swim without a shark cage. She had no means of protection from jellyfish stings that were visible on her swollen face as she emerged on the coast of Florida.

Will we all be encouraged to inquire about a major transformation occurring in the ocean presently? Warming water, rising levels, acidification and jellyfish "colonizing" the ocean again might be a cause for concern. Our existence is hinged to a healthy ocean.

Perhaps the conclusion of Gershwin's book on jellyfish will draw us from planetary passivity:

"The ancient seas were dominated by flora and fauna similar to those that today's seas appear to be shifting toward. No spectacular coral reefs. No vast filtering mussel beds. No sharks slicing through the water as menhaden multitudes flee. Just jellyfish…lots of jellyfish. It might seem outlandish and farcical to think that jellyfish could rule the seas. But they've done it before, and now we have opened the door for them to do it again. Jellyfish are weeds. They are opportunists. When they have the opportunity, taking over is probably, to some extent, just what jellyfish do."

How could jellyfish take over the ocean? "One bite at a time" Gershwin says.

"We are creating a world more like the late Precambrian (4.5 billion years ago) than the late 1800's – a world where jellyfish ruled the seas and organisms with shells didn't exist. We are creating a world where humans may soon be unable to survive, or want to."

---

[9] Ocean acidity rises in proportion to the carbon dioxide we emit into our atmosphere. Since May 2013 carbon dioxide exceeded 400 parts per million, the highest ever in human history. Please read: Ocean Acidification: The Other Climate Change Issue (American Scientist – January 2014)

In full support of Paul Dayton, quoted above, I urge everyone: "Read this book!" I found Gershwin's well researched work to be more disturbing than Rachel Carson's *Silent Spring*. Both books are about quiet threats to our future; DDT was deadly to birds, nature and soon banned in certain nations. Jellies ultimate destructive possibilities have yet to be determined. Very few seem to be talking about spreading jellyfish, unless they have been stung, or their fishing interrupted by jellies.

As fish stocks vanish
Jellyfish soon take over
Stinging all swimmers

Silent Spring by Rachel Carson was a controversial study on "the state of the Earth" by one biologist.

Is Stung![10] our best "state
Of the ocean" told through fierce
Blooming jellyfish?

Likewise the future of our vulnerable ocean remains undefined. Jellies have been around over 700 million years, making them the oldest surviving creatures on Earth. Unlike DDT, lead in paint, gasoline, tobacco, CFC's or any dangerous human creations, multiplying jellyfish are at home in the ocean and they cannot be banned.

Jellyfish alone
Survive, thrive in rising sea
Levels while we sleep

---

[10] *Stung! On Jellyfish Blooms and the Future of the Ocean*, by Lisa-ann Gershwin.

Chapter 2 - "As The Ocean Goes, So Goes The Human Race"

(Jon Bowermaster in the Introduction of Oceans)

"AMERICA STRIKES
Oil"[11] but Earth's threatened ocean
Will strike back in time

Jellies, according to Lisa-ann Gershwin, are survivors which are multiplying globally. Jellies and global warming are symbiotic twins.

"Remarkably, jellyfish may have the capacity to accelerate climate change. This can happen in two ways. Jellyfish release carbon-rich feces and mucus (poo and goo) that bacteria prefer to use for respiration, jellyfish blooms turn these bacteria into carbon dioxide factories. But jellyfish also consume vast numbers of copepods and other plankton. These creatures migrate vertically through the water column, taking in carbon-rich food and releasing it in fecal pellets, which fall to the sea floor and are buried. The plankton are thus a major means of taking carbon dioxide out of the atmosphere and oceans. If their loss occurs on a large scale, it will hasten climate change."

It behooves us to remember plankton provide over half of Earth's oxygen. The "great plankton die off" may have eliminated nearly 40 percent of these tiny floating organisms since 1950.

THE NEW YORK REVIEW OF BOOKS writer Tim Flannery adds: "There is one final impact that must be considered: "acidification of the oceans....Already our oceans are 30 percent more acidic than they were thirty years ago, and creatures with shells are suffering. In recent years, there has been a mass failure of oyster spawning off the American Northwest, and tiny snails in the Arctic and Antarctic oceans are having their shells eaten away by the acid. Jellyfish lack hard parts: it seems they will pull through the acidification crisis admirably."

In billions of years
Some massive threats to our Earth
Stare us in the face

Jacques Cousteau (1910-1997) is the most famous underwater explorer and producer of over 100 documentaries on our ocean.

In *the Human, The Octopus and the Orchid* Cousteau said, "Ecology is everyone's business." Over 100,000 French citizens once urged Cousteau to run for president of their country .He prudently rejected the invitation and maintained a full schedule trying to plead for the ocean and Earth. When he heard of a

---

[11] NATIONAL GEOGRAPHIC cover story about North Dakota and "Fracking" (November 2013)

plan to dump nuclear waste in the Mediterranean, a call went out from Cousteau to his followers inviting them to block the radioactive train from harming the Mediterranean. The train did not dump radioactive waste into what Romans called "Mare Nostrum." (Our Sea)

OUR OCEAN TREMBLES

Cousteau is an Environmental Prophet who warned "Humans now have a capacity to ruin the entire ocean." Our imaginations might transport us to one dark night in the North Sea where two huge double hull oil tankers collide, or in Titanic scenery revisited, a tanker loaded with oil strikes a drifting iceberg the size of Manhattan. One oil tanker torn asunder by an iceberg could send millions of gallons of oil into our threatened ocean. Ninety-four ships were lost in 2013 (source – Allianz Global Corporate, March 29, 2014).

If Jacques Cousteau rose
From the dead to warn humans[12]
Would we change our ways?

Washington, DC "Contrarians" and corporate heads refusing to believe prophets (Svante, Carson, Teilhard, Cousteau, Thomas Berry, and James Hansen) who warned us weather is changing are tantamount to 21st century members of the Flat Earth Society that has been deprogramming people since 1547. There are physical, clearly visible aspects of nature that cannot be denied. As ice at both poles melts with scientific certainty, the reality of icebergs breaking away and venturing out to open waters is a constant threat for vessels roaming three-fourths of the "visibly round" Earth blessed by sacred ocean water.

Standing on a Louisiana coast, it is easy to view a contour on the Gulf of Mexico and see occasional brown pelicans (the state bird) that are trying to survive amid decades of oil seeking environmental abuse. The BP/Deepwater Horizon tragedy of 2010 was checked after 85 agonizing, leaking days because of tolerable weather. The BP snafu may cost $8 billion in damages ultimately. How will inevitable drilling accidents in the Arctic be dealt with?

The wealthiest corporations in history are now preparing to exploit oil and gas in frigid Arctic regions because of our insatiable quest for energy. Endless economic growth and development demand that cheap fossil fuels buried in the 360-million year old carboniferous layer be brought forth from thousands of feet below Earth, refined, then utilized for propelling "economic prosperity" to the maximum, until the Earth is exhausted.

---

[12] Paraphrasing of the biblical parable would read:" If (humans) do not listen to ecological prophets, they will not change their ways even if someone rises from the dead." Please read (Luke 16:19)

If it was our goal
To bring down mute Earth "profit"
Is the best system[13]

Cousteau did not like
"Sustained development" on
Our finite planet

Who besides Cousteau
Would appeal faithfully for
Our dying ocean?

Earth alone will shut
Down our gross, predatory
Profit driven lives[14]

Cousteau believed "One
Continent in a life time"[15]
Yet spoke for the world

---

[13] "If it had been the design of human history to bring Earth to the edge of ruin, there is no better mechanism than the free market economy." (Kirkpatrick Sale, 1937-   )

[14] "Capitalism and militarism are two greatest sins of the 20th century."(Theologian of the social gospel, Walter Rauschenbusch, 1861-1918)

[15] Quote from THE HUMAN, THE ORCHID, THE OCTUPUS (audio disc #2)

Chapter 3 - Our Synthetic Sea

There is scientific assistance on plastic in the ocean from Captain Charles Moore of the Algalita Marine Research Center in Long Beach, California. Moore and his associates produced "*Our Synthetic Sea.*" Tiny marine organisms known as plankton are the daily diet of fish and majestic whales.

Cousteau, Captain Moore and University of Plymouth (England) marine biologist Richard Thompson have revealed facts about the ocean that do not bode well for its future; nor for humans.

> "*Richard Thompson spends a lot of time pacing Plymouth's historic edge. He especially goes in winter, when the beaches along the harbor's edge are empty. In his final year, he had 170 teammates amassing metric tons of rubbish along 85 miles of shoreline. Amid twigs and seaweed fibers in his fistful of sand are a couple of dozen blue and green cylinders about two millimeters high. They're called nurdles. They're the raw materials of plastic production. They melt down to make all kinds of things. You find these things on virtually every beach these days.*
>
> *Back in Thompson's laboratory they are finding things that are almost too small for their machine, which analyzes fragments only to twenty microns – slightly thinner than a human hair. Thompson concludes, 'That means we're underestimating the amount of plastic that we're finding. The true answer is that we just don't know how much is out there. What they do know is that there's much more than ever before.*
>
> *During the early 20th century, Plymouth marine biologist Alistair Hardy developed an apparatus that could be towed behind an Antarctic expedition boat, 10 meters below the surface, to sample krill – an ant-sized, shrimp-like invertebrate on which much of the planet's food chain rests. In the 1930's he modified it to measure even smaller plankton....Thompson's team realized that slow mechanical action-waves and tides that grind against shorelines, turning rocks into beaches – were now doing the same to plastics....At the same time, there was no sign that any of the plastic was biodegrading, even when reduced to tiny fragments.*
>
> *He knew the terrible tales of sea otters choking on polyethylene rings from beer six-packs; of swans and gulls strangled by nylon nets and fishing lines; of a green sea turtle in Hawaii dead with a pocket comb, a foot of nylon rope, and a toy truck wheel lodged in its gut. His personal worst was a study on fulmar (white seabird) carcasses washed ashore on North Sea coastlines. Ninety-five percent had plastic in their stomach, an average of 44 pieces per bird. A proportional amount in a human being would weigh nearly five pounds. 'Can you believe it?' Richard Thompson demands of no one in particular... 'They're selling plastic meant to go right down the drain, into the sewers, into the rivers, right into the ocean. Bite-size pieces of plastic to be swallowed by little sea creatures. When they get as small as powder, even zooplankton will swallow them.*" (The World Without Us, by Alan Weisman, p144-147)

Thirty-five million years ago whales morphed from creatures with four legs into sleek mammals that found their security in ocean water. In the 21st century there is growing awareness of the fact whales and the entire ocean are threatened by humans. Whales feed on plankton that provide much of Earth's decreasing supply of oxygen. Professor William Broecker of Columbia University has done extensive research on Earth's declining supply of oxygen.

"The earth's surface is 71 percent ocean and 6 percent rainforest. As we eliminate more and more rainforest, the plants (plankton) in the ocean will become increasingly important to our survival. Of course, the opposite is true; as we drive our oceans into increasingly poor condition, the rainforest becomes more and more important." *(Stung!,* p. 285)

Captain Moore and his researchers carefully measured the amount of plankton, and nodules of plastic in an area of the ocean known as the "Pacific gyre." To their amazement it was scientifically discovered plastic particles outnumbered plankton by a ratio of six to one. Marine creatures and aquatic birds have difficulty distinguishing between odorless, inert plastic nodules and plankton. Sadly, creatures in search of food end up ingesting harmful plastic pieces rather than nourishing plankton. Plastic will inevitably harm the endocrine (hormonal excretions) system of all creatures that consume it.

Did Jacques Cousteau ever envision ocean devastation surreptitiously occurring by human "plastification" of the blue water planet? Tens of thousands of plastic items per square mile can be found easily on beaches and in open waters of our life giving ocean. (Please read Thomas Hayden US NEWS & WORLD REPORT, 4 November, 2002)

Plastic – 6, Plankton – 1 is a very unwholesome imbalance for all who strive to survive on Earth, especially non-human beings which are frequently unable to distinguish what is toxic from life giving sources.

During the 1980's while hiking the Appalachian Trail in Pennsylvania I wondered how birds or animals approaching crystal clear streams would be able to protect themselves when quenching their thirst below large signs posted by US National Parks Service near streams that warned:

"DO NOT DRINK THIS WATER."

How do animals
Read warning signs saying "DO
NOT DRINK THIS WATER"?

"*Our Sacred Ocean*" is my soft, genteel line that is more bluntly, precisely articulated by marine biologist Lisa-ann Gershwin. Part IV of her book is bluntly entitled:

"THE OCEANS ARE DYING TO TELL US SOMETHING"

There is but one ocean with different geographical titles. The entire hydrological system enveloping Earth is indeed slowly dying. Scientists caution threats from blind human exploitation of Earth have never been so severe in 300 million years. Can we in the 21st century continue living as if we are the last generation?

Earth has never felt
Such rank abuse from humans
As in the present

Gershwin then documents, "The six major threats to our seas, summarized by global expert organizations, make these conclusions clear:

*OVERFISHING – According to the Food and Agriculture Organization of the United Nations (FAO, 205), for the 441 wild fish stocks globally…77 percent are fully fished or worse. Of these, 52 percent are fully exploited, 17 percent are overexploited, 7 percent are depleted and 1 percent are recovering from depletion; only 23 percent of the ocean's wild fish stocks are less than fully exploited. No other information is available on the status of the other 143 stocks.

*CLIMATE CHANGE – According to the Intergovernmental Panel on Climate Change (IPCC, 2007), 'For the next two decades a warming of about 0.2C per decade is projected for a range of SRES (reference) emissions scenarios. Even if the concentrations of all GHGs(greenhouse gases) and aerosols had been kept constant at 2000 levels, a further warming of 0.1C per decade would be expected…Anthropogenic (human induced) warming and sea level rise would continue for centuries due to the time scales associated with climate processes and feedbacks, even if GHG concentrations were to be stabilized.'

*EUTROPHICATION (overabundance of nutrients such as nitrates and phosphates) – According to the United Nations Environment Programme (UNEP, 2006), 'the potential seriousness of this problem was not seen only a few decades ago, when it was first emerging. Over the past few years, the magnitude and intractability of the problem has become apparent. Increased demand for food for an expanding global population, intensified agriculture and an estimated 2.4 – 2.7-fold increase by 2050 in nitrogen and phosphorus-driven eutrophication of terrestrial, freshwater and near-shore marine ecosystems are all elements of a worrying picture of the future.'

*OTHER POLLUTION – 'The hardest truth about the state of our marine environment is that we've trashed our ocean, the source of much of the food, water, and oxygen we need to survive. Marine debris is now considered one of the most pervasive pollution problems plaguing our ocean and waterways, and our growing population is eating more of it than ever before (*Ocean Conservancy* 2010, p16) 'The degradation time for plastic in the marine environment is, for the most part unknown. Estimates are in the region of hundreds of years.'

*PLAGUE SPECIES – According to the Global Invasive Species Programme (GISP, 2010, 5) 'Climate change will have direct and second order impacts that facilitate the introduction, establishment and/or spread of invasive species. Invasive species can increase the vulnerability of ecosystems to other climate-related stressors and also reduce the possibility to sequester greenhouse gases.'

*OCEAN ACIDIFICATION – According to *the Intergovernmental Panel on Climate Change* (IPCC, 2007, 52) 'The uptake of anthropogenic carbon since 1750 has led to the ocean becoming more acidic with an average decrease in pH of 0.1 units. Increasing atmospheric CO (2) lead to further acidification. Projections based on SRES scenarios give a reduction in average global surface ocean pH of between 0.14 and 0.35 units over the 21st century…The progressive acidification of oceans is expected to have negative impacts on marine shell-forming (e.g. corals) and their dependent species.'" (*Stung! On Jellyfish Blooms and the Future of the Ocean,* pp 338 – 340).

Gershwin adds: "It is now clear that our marine ecosystems are in free-fall due to multiple stressors, and there is no easy fix. Hell, there isn't even a hard fix. The startling truth is we screwed up. It's not a matter of cutting back on fishing…or reducing a bit on carbon emissions…or keeping an eye out for introduced species. Even if we convinced the whole world to do all of those things…it's too late."

Our oceans are the equivalent of a patient with cancer that has metastasized to six different organs. There are some things that we, wise as we are, still can't make right.

So then, what is left? After the big fish and the marine mammals have vanished, after the worms and clams have suffocated in the bottom hypoxia (no oxygen) and the snails and corals and the calcified plankton have disintegrated, after the birds and the mussels and big sea cucumbers have choked on plastic bullets, and the macroalgae have succumbed to the shading of the dinoflagellates (single-cell organisms with two flagellate), what is left?

Jellyfish

As her consciousness[16]
We continue daily to
Plead on Earth's behalf

Where life is still found[17]
There is always hope for change
If we keep breathing

Our source of hope is
Promise not to stop speaking
On behalf of Earth

For those who have neither time nor spirit to pour through Gershwin's relevant 400-page book, here are brief excerpts from the NEW YORK REVIEW OF BOOKS article:

"*Stung! On Jellyfish Blooms and the Future of the Ocean* by Lisa-ann Gershwin was featured in *The New York Review of Books* periodical, *"Their Taking Over!"* September 26, 2013). *The New York Review of Books* author Tim Flannery observed: "Then the Gulf experienced Hurricane Katrina and the oil spill of 2010. Fish and prawn numbers plummeted, but the Australian spotted jellyfish kept going from strength to strength. By 2011 jellies had shown up in the Western Mediterranean, and more than ten people a day were being stung, forcing the closure of tourist beaches in the height of the season. It's

---

[16] "We are Earth coming to consciousness." (Teilhard de Chardin)

[17] Dum anima est, spes est." ("Where there is life, there is hope." - Cicero)

recently been spotted off Israel and Brazil, from the Arctic to the equator and on to Antarctica, jellyfish plagues (or blooms) are on the increase."

Having lived in Louisiana since 1994, it is my humble feeling that survivors of Hurricane Katrina (August 2005) and the April 20, 2010 British Petroleum tragedy that killed eleven workers then leaked much oil into the Gulf would be awestruck if they read Flannery's review of *Stung!* then realized how "jellies" survived both disasters in the Gulf of Mexico.

During the horrendous "black bleeding" of Deepwater Horizon into the Gulf of Mexico I read a column by one bold journalist of this oil-dominated state who did not hesitate to mention in the Baton Rouge ADVOCATE there are 28,000 abandoned wells in the Gulf. Are they leaking? Who wishes to drill for truth when the Louisiana economy benefits handsomely from oil? Thousands of jobs are associated with oil and gas in the Louisiana area.

Senator Foster Campbell of Bossier City, Louisiana said, "They might as well put the star of TEXACO on top of the state capital building because they (energy magnates) run this state." Carving up land for pipelines means marshland will be weakened and ultimately the marsh will be lost forever to the Gulf of Mexico. In the US, there are now more square miles of land paved over than covered by rich marshland. Lacking protective marsh, hurricanes are far more destructive.

(Please read "Louisiana Agency sues dozens of energy companies for damage to wetlands" THE NEW YORK TIMES, July 25, 2013)

Environmentalist Rupert Cutler's comment on increasing loss of nature applies to Louisiana now under threat by "developers" - "Asphalt is the land's last crop."

Senator Campbell is one of the fully awake Louisiana officials who is not among "the best politicians money can buy." He speaks out for nature and challenges rather than" tap dance" (his words) with energy giants. His personal energy and enthusiasm are appreciated by environmental groups and ordinary citizens of Louisiana.

Senator Campbell knows lobbyists in the nation are aware of J.Paul Getty's advice. "If business is your profession, you better make politics your business." Our common future depends upon extricating politicians from the clutches of banking and energy business moguls in every nation.

Ken Silverstein of Harper's wrote, "In Baton Rouge I met with some of the state's most powerful lobbyists, among them Don Briggs, the cantankerous but immensely likable head of the Louisiana Oil & Gas Association, and Ginger Sawyer of the LA Association of Business and Industry, who is equally amiable but known also for toughness and savvy. Briggs and Sawyer give the industry plenty of political firepower at home.

He has been a ferocious opponent of government regulation; while she has helped oil companies win numerous tax breaks and exemptions....The battles they've fought within the state have in turn been mirrored on the national stage, with Louisiana's increasingly pro-oil congressional delegation acting as de facto industry lobbyists. This dynamic has been playing out for decades, but particularly so during the 1970's and 1980's when Louisiana politicians played key roles in winning still-extant exemptions for oil companies from federal regulations imposed by Congress in response to public concern about the environment. A 1989 New Orleans TIMES PICAYUNE story estimated that American oil companies collectively saved $6.7 billion annually thanks to the exemption."(This) does not make sense from an environmental perspective," a government official said anonymously to the newspaper. "Oil interests …wanted the exemption. They got the exemption."

Coming from Illinois, I am always learning more about this fascinating state and how vital it is to the continental USA. Walking to a nearby exercise facility in 2012, I encountered a friendly Cajun man who detected my accent was not native to Louisiana. After telling him my Illinois history, he asked if I ever heard of Henry, LA and the "Henry Hub." I was ignorant. He explained that the Henry Hub was one of the top ten KGB targets during the Cold War because the price of natural gas was determined by the strategic location of pipelines clustered near Erath, LA. If the "Hub" was taken out by a surgical Soviet attack, energy for the entire nation would be crippled.

Silverstein highlights the timid politicians of 2013 by comparing them to the famous Long family. "It's a long way from the days of Huey Long, who as Louisiana's governor from 1928 to 1932 was the last state executive to truly confront oil interests. Long tapped into widespread resentment against big business, especially Standard Oil and its allies in the political establishment. "If they got to leave," he said after Standard Oil threatened to cease operating in the state, 'they can go to hell and stay there.'"

The political and economic elite tried to impeach Long after he proposed a five-cent-per-barrel tax on the production of refined oil to help fund social programs but he fought them off with the support of the poor and went on to be elected as a U.S. senator, serving for a year before being assassinated by the son-in-law of a political enemy." Silverstein concludes the Harper's article with some eminently practical advice from LA Democrat J. Bennett Johnson for politicians who wish to survive in Louisiana."

There are some things you can do with your states, and some things you can't. In Louisiana…you got to be pro-oil and gas….. Republican Senator David Vitter has led attacks on the EPA (for trying to place limits on carbon dioxide emissions) ….Mary Landrieu was one of only four Democrats in the US Senate to join with Republicans last year to preserve $24 billion in oil industry tax breaks tax (Please read *On Brining and Dining: How pro-oil LA politicians have shaped American environmental policy*, Harper's Magazine, October 23, 2013).

Chapter 4 - Cars, Conspiracy, Carbon Footprints

Baton Rouge and Lafayette, Louisiana are extremely congested cities with a glut of cars driving motorists to distraction. I once wrote a letter to the Baton Rouge ADVOCATE, simply pointing out the USA in the 1940's was served by good public transportation in the form of trolleys from the west coast up to New York City. Such service even included the small town of New Iberia, LA. However, the conspiracy following WW II between Standard Oil of New Jersey (EXXON), Firestone and General Motors began to pull out trolley service in California cities, then replace public transportation by selling GM busses to the cities. The illegal deprivation of public transportation from the west coast on to the Atlantic seaboard states continued under corporate chicanery. Returning to some form of decent public transportation might alleviate the gridlock of Louisiana cities, and everywhere else in the nation.

One of the ADVOCATE editors phoned to verify my letter and asked why I used the word "conspiracy". I calmly replied it was common knowledge for every legal student to know about the "GM conspiracy." to eliminate trolleys and introduce GM busses. The editor said he approved the letter but did not like that use of "conspiracy." The letter was published in a leading paper of the state, but without conspiratorial reference to the three powerful corporations, Standard Oil, Firestone and General Motors. Conspiracy simply means "breathing together" in trying to wreak injustice, if not criminal activities. As I read the letter eventually printed in THE ADVOCATE, lacking that forthright term of conspiracy, I thought of the maxim, "Whose bread I eat, his (her) song I sing." Editors do not want to bump heads with corporate CEO's even if they were clearly involved in less than honorable activities. A post card from New Iberia, LA is an oil painting of trolley tracks in New Iberia. Those tracks are solidly paved over in 2014.

If the Keystone XL pipeline is approved, powerful politicians from the energy states of Texas, Alaska, Oklahoma, Wyoming and Louisiana will have contributed much to a giant step backwards in our environmental history. Tar sands oil will inevitably contribute more carbon dioxide into our atmosphere.

Pathocracy[18] has
Assumed governance among
Sleepwalking people

The Medici family ruled Florence, Italy for three hundred years under a family coat of arms: "Money to buy power. Power to control money."

---

[18] A system of government by which a small pathological group has assumed power over the non-reflective majority.

Obsessed with power
Cash, sports to quell our boredom
Empire muddles on

Wall Street bailout
Removed Four point six trillion ($4.6T)[19]
From sleeping "sheeple[20]

NUCLEAR SACRIFICE ZONE

While several of us were personally expressing opposition (then arrested by the State Police) to environmental devastation at the US Department of Energy's (DOE) nuclear test site in Nevada, I heard sacred Shoshone Native American Nevada territory described as our "Nuclear sacrifice zone." A 200-mile tour of the nuclear test site conducted by a DOE guide was our risky exposure to radioactivity. The deadly nuclear rays were clicking out of the Geiger counter held by Canadian epidemiologist Sister Rosalie Bertell. (1929-2012). Large craters in the desert indicated where underground detonations occurred making the Shoshone desert radioactive forever. Young women in our group of nuclear opponents who had hopes of bearing children in the future were advised by Sr. Rosalie to skip our ride through a ruined, deadly desert.

Without question we
Are the foremost empire since
Collapsed Roman times

Country destroying
Nuclear weapons[21] assure
Power over all

TOXIC SACRIFICE ZONE?

Some forthright residents of Louisiana have described their own violated state as a "Toxic sacrifice zone" in moments of brutal honesty I never heard before. Senator Campbell is not one to retreat from powerful corporate figures in Louisiana. May his strength, courage and alertness long endure for the sake of this state used by gas, petroleum and chemical companies as Louisiana's economic life support systems. Without doubt oil, gas and chemicals have brought thousands of jobs and prosperity to many in Louisiana. However, this state is tied with Mississippi for last place in areas such as health care, poverty, high in illiteracy. Just how long will dubious prosperity extend into the future of a warming

---

[19] AllGov (Everything our government really does) April 5, 2010 (please **see www.allgov.com**) The Wall Street bailout came mostly from Federal Reserve loans. None of the Wall Street executives have been convicted of criminal activity. Only Bernard Madoff (1938 -   ) was convicted of fraud and now serving time. He may be free from threats by many whose investments he lost. (Please see *Inside Story* for a history of the 2008 global financial collapse).

[20] Satirical term of people resembling sheep, coined by radio commentator William Cooper (1943-2001), author of *Behold a Pale Horse*, who predicted the 9/11 event.

[21] The US and Russia have over 90 percent of an estimated 17,700 country-destroying nuclear weapons in 2014. All five members of the UN Security Council (Britain, China, France, Russia, and USA) hypocritically cling to their weapons while trying to stop proliferation among Gulf nations other than Israel. Israel still denies having such weapons. President Truman was the only head of state to authorize use of atomic weapons on August 6th and 9th 1945. Can we prevent the third use?

planet? Visiting hurricanes are painful reminders for all that transition to our obtaining renewable sources of energy must occur eventually.

Breaking more records[22]
Warming Earth is begging us
End fossil fuels

Are we Earth coming
Into awareness of what
We do to ourselves?

In addition to normal recommended sleep of eight hours, Louisiana citizens devote much quality time to family, food, fishing, festivals and football. Busy citizens of this state are not often reminded Louisiana soil   floats into the Gulf at a steady pace.

A teachable moment might be realized in the New Orleans Saints (Mercedes Benz) stadium or Louisiana State University (LSU) Tiger Stadium if one of the famous quarterbacks or coaches seized the microphone and told thousands of football fans at half time to imagine the entire football field suddenly being swallowed up by the Gulf of Mexico – forever. That is exactly what is occurring in the state every thirty minutes 24 hours a day.

Forget such a personal fantasy .Football is not a contact sport; it is a "collision sport" gone amok. New Orleans Saints and Tigers football seem to "narcotize" Louisiana. The highest paid public figure in the state is LSU football coach Les Miles at $4.3 million yearly. Miles ranks #5 in the nation. Does such an obsession indicate football may dominate university education? When Fr. Theodore Hesburgh expressed a desire to end football at Notre Dame University, alumni members warned they would not give any more money to Notre Dame. Football survives in 2014. Do sporting events and shopping have a similar numbing effect on the entire nation? A clue can be found in chapters of *Friendly Fascism* written in 1980 by Bertram Gross.

---

[22] More than 6,000 records were broken in 2012

New Orleans parties[23]
With shallow awareness they
Are slowly drowning[24]

In 1992, 1,700 professors as members of the Union of Concerned Scientists issued a warning that humankind, like colliding football players, was on a "collision course with the planet" if we do not change our relationship. Ecological collision is evident through the fact millions of people globally live in areas that are only three feet above high tide. As the celebrations progress, eighty percent of US coastal erosion takes place on the Louisiana coastline.

Can we strive to imagine what we already know about the rising ocean?

Roman emperors constructed stadiums in all colonies from Syria to Britain where the gladiator games ("Circus Maximus") were held to keep citizens unaware of a collapsing empire. The Roman coliseum held around 50,000 people. LSU's Tiger Stadium has a capacity over 93,000. In 2014 the capacity will be increased to 103,000. The University of Alabama in 2013 has a capacity of 103,000. Penn State in 2013 is the largest with 109,000. The largest football stadiums are on university campuses, not in impoverished areas of US cities where professional teams play. The drawing power of modern sporting events is similar to the crafty design of Roman emperors who had to keep citizens of the empire distracted from reality.

Speaking out against oil industry perks or for protection of the environment in Louisiana can be risky, as Huey Long discovered.

Wilma Subra is a respected scientist who dares to challenge a corporate rush to plunder this state's portion of our planet. There is a bullet hole in the wall of her New Iberia office. Wilma also serves as a consultant for Louisiana Environmental Action Network (LEAN)

Mary Lee Orr, assisted by her two sons, is the executive director of LEAN, a 27-year old environmental organization based in Baton Rouge. Wilma Subra and Mary Lee Orr are two of my heroines in the endless struggle to protect Earth from those who pillage our precious planet.

---

[23] A protest against the KEYSTONE XL pipeline was held in New Orleans on September 21, 2013. Physically unable to walk six blocks amid heavy car and buggy traffic with one semi-paralyzed leg, I peacefully sat by the famous CAFÉ DU MONDE in the French Quarter. I watched tourists stand in line and wait patiently for seats in the crowded restaurant. Without seeking permission from staff members, pigeons and sparrows assumed their place at tables in the restaurant to clean off leftovers after tourists finished their coffee and beignets. Since I had no ticket for the scheduled 3PM wedding, security guards would not allow me to find quiet in the historic St. Louis Cathedral near Jackson Square. Hundreds of celebrating tourists ate, drank, attended weddings and simply enjoyed a taste of New Orleans only a short distance from the mighty, temperamental, Mississippi that could send everybody running for cover if another Katrina visits.

[24] In addition to being twelve feet below a rising Atlantic, New Orleans is slowly sinking.

"Women hold up half
The sky"[25] in each nation with
Loving compassion

Nothing but bullets
Will prevent lovers of Earth
From speaking their minds

Be "coffin ready"[26]
Is practical advice for
All living beings

Harold Schoeffler of Lafayette has been the most prominent voice for our Sierra Club in Lafayette. Harold is a walking environmental encyclopedia who has probably paddled most of the rivers and bayous in Louisiana. Harold hosts "Ecologic" a monthly Lafayette (Acadiana Open Channel AOC) cable television program. Harold reminds us there is but one paid lobbyist for the Sierra Club in Baton Rouge versus dozens who represent industry. Lobbyists are "assigned" to meet with each elected official in the state.

Sarah Schoeffler is a generous volunteer in the community and advocate for Trees of Acadiana. Sarah and Harold Schoeffler are prominent "voices for our Earth community."

Haywood "Woodie" Martin is a tireless worker for the Sierra Club and editor of the DELTA CHAPTER newsletter.

Steve Landry from Franklin, LA has been fishing, bringing in shrimp and crabs since his youth. In recent decades he observed how water quality and wild life in Louisiana bayous have declined. Shrimping and fishing have become more difficult with increasing incursions of jellyfish in local waters. Those who catch shrimp and fish know from experience what is occurring. At one time Steve dipped his T-shirt in the Mississippi, then squeezed the water into his mouth to slake his thirst. Game wardens in 2013 warned him, "Do not even think of that now!"

Those who fish for a living are busy trying to care for their families in one of the poorest states. They do not have time in their boats to read much about what is happening to our environment, nor do they have time to write books or send letters to local newspapers. Struggling fisher folk are only trying to survive. All can be grateful to Lisa Gershwin for revealing more about disturbing ecological trends.

---

[25] Chinese proverb

[26] Quote from M.L. King, Jr.

Chapter 5 - Jellies Are Indeed Taking Over The Ocean

"Tierny Thys is one of the world's experts on Mola Mola, the giant ocean sunfish. But her love, understanding of, and curiosity about the importance of all fishes is boundless." *(Oceans* by Jon Bowermaster)

Thys corroborates Lisa-ann Gershwin's dire analysis of the ocean's health and invasion by multiplying jellyfish.

"We've perpetuated oceanic felonies many times over, and our seas are hemorrhaging life. Most of our technological advances have not been kind to the world of fishes. Until recently, we were able to increase our annual catch each year by perfecting our fishing gear. Not so today. The fish just aren't there. We've decimated so many of our big commercial fish stocks, such as Atlantic swordfish, blue fin tuna, and cod, that even if we stopped fishing today, populations would still take decades to rebuild. Some will never rebuild. When these large commercial species are fished out, smaller bait fishes become our next target. And when they are fished out, the whole system unravels. With fewer fish, low energy animals such as jellies can bloom in great numbers then gain a stronghold on the sea....However, report after report attests to a rising tide of jellies infiltrating our waters globally from the Bering Sea to Australia, from Japan to the coast of Africa's Namibia.

Recently, a ten-ton Japanese trawler sank when fishermen attempted to haul up too many giant Nomura jellies. Nomura jellies are exploding in numbers here, ruining reams of fishing gear and even clogging up and shutting down nuclear power plants. Jelly blooms have recently shut down beaches in Australia and the Mediterranean as well, costing the tourism industry there hundreds of millions of dollars. Off the coast of Ireland, jelly blooms have destroyed valuable salmon farms. In my home state of California, massive jelly blooms clogged intake pipes at the Diablo Canyon power plant, causing a temporary plant shutdown." (*Oceans*, p. 140)

"Diablo" in Spanish means "devil." Perhaps jellies are mean spirited marine creatures that will accomplish more than Greenpeace or any environmental organization striving to shut down nuclear power.

The Fukushima tsunami of March 2011 remains a radioactive threat in 2014 to Japanese residents and fish in the Pacific region. When radioactivity is released it must settle somewhere. If not on inert surfaces, then it will find a resting place on human or non-human flesh. Neither Tokyo Electric Power Company (TEPCO), nor the government of Japan, are able to reduce threats of radioactivity coming from the crippled nuclear plant near Fukushima (means "Island of Blessings"). In January 2014 TEPCO's leaking operation in Fukushima still bewilders nuclear experts trying to reduce releases of deadly REMs (Roentgen Equivalent Man, a measure of radioactivity) into the atmosphere. Daily monitoring reports are available.

Will jellyfish be like cockroaches that are not harmed by radioactivity? We know personally dentists record each appointment when our teeth are x-rayed. At the time of x-raying teeth patient's bodies are shielded by a heavy lead blanket while the technician scampers for safety outside the examination room. How else can we perceive the deadly nature of radioactivity?

Ironically, Pacific winds make radioactivity more threatening to the Hawaiian Islands and mainland USA than Japan. Radioactive water flowing from the disabled Fukushima nuclear plant into the Pacific on Japan's coast is having an unknown effect on fishing there.

"If you calculate the amount of Cesium 137 in the pool at Unit #4, the amount is equivalent to 14,000 Hiroshima bombs (Hiroaki Koide, professor at Kyoto Research Reactor Institute).

The 1945 bomb that destroyed Hiroshima was a small 20 kiloton (20,000 ton) device. Nuclear arsenals in 2013 include megaton (millions of tons) devices. One megaton is a freight train stretching from Kansas City, MO, 300 miles east to St. Louis, loaded with TNT (Trinitrotoluene) for our comprehension. May such weapons not be used the third time.

Those who follow events in Fukushima closely are pressing for an international effort to cope with the tragedy three years after the wounded plant still threatens Earth. (Harvey Waserman, THE PROGRESSIVE, October 8, 2013).

In a 2012 interview with Lou Dubose of THE WASHINGTON SPECTATOR, Waserman spoke forcefully: "Our survival depends upon burying all fossil fuels, and ending nuclear power."

Fortunately, a powerful cyclone missed Fukushima in October 2013.

The BBC reported on October 21, 2013 that the Fukushima nuclear mishap will be dealt with by 2017. Authorities with TEPCO and the Japanese government did not disclose to what part of Earth radioactive debris would be safely removed.

We in the USA should not feel relieved because Japan is 10,000 miles away. Hurricane Sandy (October 30, 2012) put thirty-four nuclear reactors of the USA from Maine to Florida in harm's way. (NUKEWATCH QUARTERLY, Winter 2012).

Are jellies and tsunamis "double teaming" to shut down nuclear power plants that are precariously close to shorelines? Neptune, a Roman god of the ocean still serves as a mythical divine force to protect our ocean. Followers of Gaia view Earth as a living being and our mighty ocean as simply defending the cosmos from intruding, insensitive humans.

Chapter 6 - Revealing Jail Secrets Kept Quiet For Nine Years

Louisiana is still struggling to recover from the 2005 damage left by Katrina and the April 20, 2010 British Petroleum (now ½ USA- owned) tragedy in the Gulf of Mexico. Litigation over environmental damage to our precious Gulf drags on in April 2014. Who can predict an end?

Behind closed legal doors in Louisiana secret discussions may be still occurring over cruel neglect of prisoners during Katrina. It is not likely there are many lawyers scrambling to speak for "marginal people" (economic poor who were incarcerated) in New Orleans before, during and after Katrina.

There are over a dozen correctional facilities in the city of New Orleans.

Reporting as chaplain in the Lafayette Parish Correctional Center (LPCC),the Sunday following Katrina's devastating invasion of New Orleans, I arrived by 7:30AM at the lone correctional center for adults in Lafayette to prepare for usual church services held in our humble third floor Chapel of Hope . A serious looking Lieutenant Joseph Miller, the officer assigned as supervisor for that day called me to the side and said: "I first need 150 bibles for inmates brought over from New Orleans following the hurricane that flooded the city." I told him respectfully it would not be possible to find 150 bibles on a weekend.

"Secondly," the lieutenant continued, I want you to prepare Sunday church services for inmates brought over last night." Since the next day was a holiday, I offered to return on Monday and hold church services for the forlorn "New Orleans guests" in the open LPCC basketball court. Fire regulations would surely not permit squeezing 150 more persons into one small crowded chapel designed for only fifty who wished to have a prayer service.

To complicate our lives more following the storm, the roof had been blown off a jail in the nearby town of Abbeville, LA. Inmates from that leaking facility were also brought to Lafayette. It was the first time since beginning in 2000 that I found sleep-deprived men napping in plastic boats on the chapel floor. Other "Climate refugees" from New Orleans flowed freely into Lafayette following the worst natural disaster to hit the USA. Those who escaped Katrina were scattered as far as Utah. Will the "Let the good times roll" spirit of New Orleans, be transported to Mormon country? Evacuees from New Orleans still remain in Lafayette, other cities in Louisiana and distant states in 2014. Some will not go back to NOLA for fear of storms that will eventually return to inundate "The Big Easy."

Adrenalin Of Drowning Men Breaks Down Jail Doors

Following Monday's open air church services and bible distribution to 150 inmates brought from New Orleans, I sallied forth to visit each man privately. Female inmates from New Orleans may have been transported to several other facilities for women in the state. The top floor of the crowded Lafayette Parish Correctional Center is set aside for women. In sweltering Louisiana heat, it is the most uncomfortable floor, despite air conditioning. Again, authorities will take advantage of "female docility."

Not wanting any personal involvement in legal issues or unpleasant disclosures to local journalists of what occurred as floodwaters rose in New Orleans, I did not speak to others of stressful visits to rescued/saved inmates until after mandatory medical retirement from LPCC in 2008. Opening heavy jail doors daily had begun to disable my only functioning right hand. After two operations on my right hand I followed the hand surgeon's orders to leave LPCC or "get a doorman." Later a Lafayette disability lawyer and her husband visited one day in 2008. They both urged me to retire and avoid becoming an "invalid" without use of both hands.

Now I am outside of the jail and feel free to express myself.

I visited emotionally stunned inmates from New Orleans who told of being herded into more spacious holding areas of one jail where deputies locked them in and then fled as "keepers of the keys." Katrina's rising contaminated water was quickly ankle-deep in one facility. The 8th Ward was affected more than other areas of New Orleans. No one knew how long Katrina would batter the city, already twelve feet below sea level. Nor did everyone in the city know the levees had been breached. Not even experts from the Weather Channel would predict how high water might rise from the storm surge. As toxic water rose above the ankles of inmates, panic began to grip them. Trapped inmates hoped deputies would return to set them free from drowning miserably in filthy, putrid water behind bars. No such luck.

Deputies knew their own chances of survival were outside of a doomed jail. New Orleans deputies fled the hapless scene. Inmates were left to fend for themselves as the foul water whipped up by Katrina, continued to rise. I became angry upon hearing stories from trapped inmates who were coldly abandoned in New Orleans. It was because of such harrowing survival tales that I continued visiting all potential drowning victims. They had no idea of family deaths or survivors in NOLA. The inmates were happy to be alive, even if still incarcerated in Lafayette. Water soaked jail records were lost in the storm, obfuscating their possibility of early release for time already served in New Orleans.

During those post-Katrina visits with the survivors I was told how inmates finally gave up hope of seeing deputies return to release them from their rising watery tomb. Who can scientifically measure the pounds per square inch (psi) strength of doomed prisoners trapped behind jail doors with oily flood waters drawing slowly closer to their mouths? It was explained quite vividly how trapped inmates simply combined all their adrenalin-driven strength into a phalanx of power to break down the jail door or doors that would soon seal their horrible slow drowning. Rupturing themselves or injuring discs in their backs trying to break down the jail door seemed better than passively drowning behind bars. In a screaming explosion of adrenalin, desperate inmates broke out of their "gated community." Once back out in the streets of NOLA, authorities were probably waiting in police cruisers to arrest them again amid the utter chaos of a city under siege by Katrina.

Years later I am finally relating to others what was told to me by surviving inmates. I am secretly applauding their bold escape from certain death. I will never be able to mentally eradicate their tales of survival from within submerging penal facilities. Why must I keep this harrowing drama a secret? Who follows lives of 150 inmates that were fortunate enough to break out of jail confinement to find a degree of freedom? Jail officers who fled, knowing abandoned inmates would soon drown must live with their collective conscience. Deputies too probably have pulled out of New Orleans, suspecting another hurricane will again visit one year. Then the pumps that keep the city from drowning might be overwhelmed and fail. No one can lock deputies in that city surrounded by a rising Atlantic, Lake Borgne, Lake Pontchartrain on the north and a mighty Mississippi almost looming above parts of New Orleans. No semi-conscious urban planner would have chosen to locate a major city in such watery surroundings.

German settlers in the 1720's were moved into an area above present day New Orleans. Native Americans were in North America for thousands of years before Europeans arrived. They were using the location above New Orleans as a trading post according to historians.

Estimates of those who died or vanished during Katrina range from 1900 to 2500. Nobody claims to know with any accuracy. My personal desire/prayer for 150 surviving inmates encountered in LPCC is that they remain far from penal institutions. And that there never be anything like Katrina to strike Louisiana again. Will we ever know a number for dead or missing victims?

Chapter 7 - You Gotta See It Happen In LPCC!

It was initially difficult to visualize inmates soon to drown simply break down jail doors. Of course I could not personally verify what actually occurred in the New Orleans "break out." The dramatic escape event was later personally reinforced by a display of strength in one very unusual day of the Lafayette jail.

Only once in eight years did I see LPCC deputies run in fear from an inmate. A young, emaciated blonde woman was undergoing painful "detoxing" from her drug/alcohol addictions. The unspeakable power of adrenalin was again verified as the angry, suffering woman pulled a metal toilet from the wall of her confined detoxification area. She broke out of the enclosure with the toilet then chased four deputies down the hall threatening to punish them with the metal toilet she was brandishing above her agonizing, frail Cajun body.

The first of four frightened officers was running fastest while carrying a large plastic shield for protection. He called for assistance, screaming, "Send help, she has a weapon" (the metal toilet seat) with which she threatened to bash the fleeing deputies. Pepper spray is the only weapon carried by jail staff members. For eight good years I relied on faithful guardian angels! Never was I threatened by an inmate. Completely awestruck by the ongoing detoxing escape I stepped back into a guard's protected enclosure with three prospective jail volunteers. Soon a torrent of water flowed down the hall after the toilet had been physically pulled from its large pipeline and wall moorings. Safely inside the floor deputy's guard post, four of us witnessed the chase by an infuriated woman and mini flood that followed her unique display of physical strength. In an instant, three possible volunteers including Michael Doucet, a famous Cajun musician, and one veteran airline hostess withdrew their generous offers to help out in the jail. They had seen enough of LPCC life in one visit. Winnie, the airline worker was trained for plane crashes, but not for dangerous "adrenalin rushes" of an angry woman who displayed strength beyond our imagination.

With such an incredible exhibition of lone female bare handed strength, the dramatic story of trapped inmates about to drown in New Orleans became more believable to me.

Chapter 8 - Are We All Trapped Inmates?

Most analogies limp, but are we not all prisoners of our warming ocean as it continues to rise globally? It appears we are all symbolically, ontologically imprisoned like NOLA inmates. Is it not powerful fossil fuel industries and CEO's who deny climate change?

Have the "movers and shakers" of fossil fuel corporations swayed the judgments of elected officials on climate and collectively locked all on Earth within an enclosure that is transfixed by carbon dioxide fueling our warming, rising ocean? Do powerful politicians and energy CEO's not hold the keys of our warming, watery imprisonment? Those who may have retired to luxurious condominiums in Miami will find their property values go down soon as the Atlantic rises to claim the vulnerable "sunshine" state.

Global "FRACKDOWN" (**www.globalfrackdown.org**) held on October 19, 2013 manifested willingness to block hydraulic fracturing ("fracking") that is wasting millions of gallons of water already in short supply. (Please view GASLAND 1 and 2 by Josh Fox). Fracking will be going global if we do not soon perceive the extent of damage it causes to our environment.

Does not undefined
Subconscious grief flow from our
Perishing planet?

Without a cosmic
Consciousness we will be lost
In the fossil age

Vermont was the first US state to ban hydraulic fracturing. France banned fracking in June 2011. Bulgaria and parts of Spain also banned the process. Will millions of citizens globally realize water is more important to our future than oil? Will we rise to demand an end to the wasteful, destructive, toxic hydraulic fracturing practice?

With some European bans on fracking, US energy corporations shrewdly viewed the move to ban fracking as an opportunity to sell more gas from North America. In corporate meetings, we notice bottled water is usually visible on large board room tables as an indicator of little trust placed in local water purity. Bottled water companies in a multi-billion dollar business are not required to check quality. Lafayette does daily checks for water purity.

FORBES 500 yearly provides information on the top global economic powers. Among the top 150, 59% are corporations, not countries. The top ten economic entities are dominated by energy corporations which have imprisoned us into a global fossil fuel economy. CEO's of Munich Reh, an insurance corporation, note "weather events" are costing insurance companies billions more since the 1950's. They know fossil fuels are to blame. "Power versus power" might eventually pit insurance goliaths against obtuse corporate energy bosses.

EXXON MOBIL CEO Rex Tillerson admits global warming is a problem we have caused. However, with an income of $100,000 daily he concludes, "We will adapt." Will we really? Can Tillerson retain his executive status for such honesty? In the 1990's Sir John Browne told an audience in Los Angeles,

"The age of oil is over!" Thomas Berry refers to the "Petroleum Interval" in one chapter of his book *The Great Work.*

India, in Tillerson's trend of thought has already begun "adaptation" to a rising Bay of Bengal by building a 4,000 mile wall on the southern border with Bangladesh. Government officials in Delhi claim it is for protection against "terrorists." However, perceptive environmental observers envision a future when thousands of "climate refugees" in low-lying Bangladesh will be forced to flee from ocean flooding. They will travel north to India, rather than remain "imprisoned" then drowned by rising waters from the Bay of Bengal.

Chapter 9 - Sixth Great Extinction?

Elizabeth Kolbert, wrote *The Sixth Great Extinction?* for THE NEW YORKER (May 25, 2009). Kolbert and Harvard biologist E.O. Wilson, along with other scientists, conclude there have been five great die-offs in history. This time, the cataclysm is ourselves, brought on by our blind environmental misbehavior. (Please read *The Diversity of Life* by E.O. Wilson, p32) In addition to Kolbert's NEW YORKER article she wrote *Field Notes from a Catastrophe* in 2006.

The Age of Stupid is a lengthy documentary that summarizes better than any how we have ventured into an unforgiving, warming age from which we must try to retreat soon. Withdrawing from fossil fuels may be within our capacity, if scales fall from eyes of "keepers of the keys" in corporate board rooms and government offices.

"Some estimates suggest that, if current trends continue, half of the world's species may disappear by the end of this century." (Kolbert, THE NEW YORKER) Are humans admitting to being among endangered species?

Who on planet Earth
Will find relief from global
Warming, climate change?

In 2014, Kolbert wrote *"The Sixth Extinction."* On her book cover, as ominously different from her May 25, 2009 NEW YORKER contribution there was no question mark (?). Has her outlook regarding our environmental awareness changed in five years?

The cover of NATIONAL GEOGRAPHIC (September 2013) depicts the Statue of Liberty with water surrounding her waist. "Rising Seas" is the theme with articles and graphs that warn of our future. Most striking is the prognosis for Asia: "Land, now inhabited by 600 million Chinese would flood, as would all of Bangladesh, population, 160 million, and much of coastal India. The inundation of the Mekong Delta would leave Cambodia's Cardamom Mountains stranded as an island." We who are concerned about our rising ocean and future generations will find the NATIONAL GEOGRAPHIC issue help us to imagine what we already know about the warming ocean that must expand.

In mid-October 2013 a cyclone, the size of Katrina struck the Bay of Bengal. In the same week dozens of economic refugees from Africa died in trying to reach the Mediterranean island of Lampedusa. Victims paid dearly for escape to Europe with hopes of finding a better life there.

As our rising ocean threatens millions living too close to the shore, will there be enough islands like Lampedusa for temporary safety?

Some of the most vulnerable areas in the USA are New Orleans and Miami. NATIONAL GEOGRAPHIC researchers continue: "New Orleans may be safe for a few decades, but the long-term prospects for it and other low-lying cities look dire. Among the most vulnerable is Miami. 'I cannot envision southeastern Florida having many people at the end of this century' says Hal Wanless, chairman of the department of geological sciences at the University of Miami. We're sitting in his basement office, looking at maps of Florida on his computer. At each click of the mouse, the years pass, the ocean rises, and the peninsula shrinks. With seas four feet higher than they are today – a distinct possibility by 2100 – about two-thirds of southeastern Florida will be inundated. The Florida Keys have almost vanished. Miami is an island." (NATIONAL GEOGRAPHIC, September 2013, p. 55)

Not featured in the NG article are prospects for the world's largest naval base in Norfolk, VA. To where can the invincible naval base be moved? (Please read THE DAILY CLIMATE, November 2, 2013.) The Atlantic is already encroaching upon homes in Norfolk. The fifth-term Mayor Paul Fraim is seeking funds to prepare for the inevitable. He wishes to raise streets and sewers to cope with a soggy future. Norfolk is surrounded by the Atlantic, the Chesapeake Bay and James River. In the last century the ocean has risen from five to eight inches. Like New Orleans, Norfolk is also sinking. Is the rising ocean/sinking land double threat is a possible future for other cities along coastlines?

November 8, 2013 the central region of Philippine islands were slammed by the most powerful winds ever recorded. The Tondo area of Manila is a six hectare slum and perhaps the largest congestion of shacks in Asia. Flimsy structures will not survive winds over 100 miles per hour.

Chapter 10 - We Were Warned 100 Years Ago About Fossil Fuels

(Our first clear warning came in 1890.)

Hundred year[27] learning
Curves will not protect children
From global warming

By the 1980's scientists began to pay closer attention. NASA scientist James Hansen dared to speak first to "environmentally dozing" government leaders in Washington.

Will hostility
Of Earth toward humans now
Be our learning time?

Thirty year[28] learning
Curves among officials lead
US toward dead ends

Salvation Today Includes Earth

"Do not harm the land or the sea until we have put our God's seal on the foreheads of the faithful!" (Revelation 7:3) Religious leaders of our era are slowly beginning to "read the signs of the times." "The task of bishops is to read the signs of the times."(St. Irenaeus, 130-200)

Hildegard of Bingen (1098-1179) and Julian of Norwich (1342-1416) were centuries ahead in appreciating the beauties and importance of nature.

Augustine of Hippo (354-430) may have experienced life with beauties of Earth in North Africa before Romans clear cut trees for building their world conquering ships. Even the Sahara was once covered with trees and vegetation. Now desertification spreads faster than ever recorded in 10,000 years of human history.

---

[27] Svante August Arrhenius (1859-1927), is a Swedish scientist and one of the founders of physical chemistry. A Nobel Peace Prize was given to him in 1903. In 1890 Arrhenius warned us unlimited burning of fossil fuels will eventually be harmful to Earth.

[28] On June 24, 1988 NASA scientist James Hansen told the US Congress, it was 99 percent certain "Global warming is a reality." In 2014 (as mentioned previously) nearly half of elected officials are vocal "contrarians" who still deny climate change/global warming. Scorned by some government cohorts, the prophetic Hansen retired from NASA in 2012 with hopes of devoting himself to environmental education efforts. Will those in Washington open their minds when a rising Potomac River floods the capitol and causes plumbing in government buildings to back up? All who live in New York vividly recall hurricanes Irene in 2011 and Sandy in 2012 that shut down New York City and did damage along the entire Atlantic coast. A closed stock exchange remembers.

"I asked the earth, the sea and the deeps, heaven, the sun, the moon and the stars…My questioning of them was my contemplation, and their answer was their beauty...They do not change their voice, that is their beauty, if one person is there to see and another to see and to question...Beauty appears to all in the same way, but it is silent to one and speaks to the other…They understand it who compare the voice received on the outside with the truth that lies within." (Confessions of St. Augustine, pp. 234-35)

Jesuit mystic and paleontologist Teilhard de Chardin (1881 -1955) was decades ahead of his time in declaring, "We are Earth coming to consciousness." (Quoted earlier)

Earth took on body	*Teilhard Chardin was*
With soul in us to revere	*Prophet, priest, poet to those*
Her awesome beauty	*Who loved his wisdom*

In the early 1990's a $4-million ecumenical effort entitled "Renewing the Earth" occurred among major Christian denominations to raise care of Earth to a higher level. THE WALL STREET JOURNAL (WSJ) was one of the few major newspapers that took note of churches speaking out for the planet. WSJ editors were critical of such involvement by religious bodies. Could it be that spiritual leaders speaking in defense of our environment would curtail growth in the profit system?

The website, **www.catholicclimatecovenant.org** is available for all who appreciate pure air, water, decent food in our threatened environment. All denominations are beginning to take note of our collective responsibility to protect the planet from devastation.

After Noah's bold
Venture[29] there are no arks in
Which we can escape

The Fate of Mountain Glaciers in the Anthropocene was published by the Pontifical Academy of Sciences in Rome on May 11, 2011. Anthropocene is defined as the "human-made geologic epoch in which we now live." (P3 of a 15-page research paper on 400 vanishing mountain glaciers.) "If we want justice and peace, we must protect the habitat that sustains us," the Vatican document concludes.

More than anyone
In our Anthropocene age
Earth is crucified

While attempting environmental awareness programs for Maryknoll (Catholic Foreign Mission Society of America, based at Ossining, NY) beginning in the Dallas, San Antonio and Houston areas, I was thoroughly bothered by the unsightly Houston Ship Channel and its toxic threats to the Gulf of Mexico. A haiku on the Gulf bubbled up in my consciousness during 1989. Functioning as a member of Maryknoll, the Catholic Foreign Mission Society of America (legal title), it was important for me to link care of Earth to the Gospel:

---

[29] Genesis chapters 6 – 9

"Don't swear by heaven, for it is God's throne; don't swear by Earth for it is God's footstool." (Matthew 5:35) Are we not presently talking about salvation of Earth? Jesus lived in pre-industrial times. However, our 21st century message may be newly formatted within the pulverizing industrial / technological / digital / military ice age.

Win the world for Christ　　　　　　　　*Salvation cannot*
Lose our Gulf of Mexico　　　　　　　　*Be isolated from one's*
Just what have we gained?　　　　　　　*Survival on Earth*

"Go tell the Good News"
Salvation depends on care
Of Pacha Mama[30]

During an environmental visit to El Salvador in 1994, Dr. Ricardo Navarro (holder of PhD's from Purdue and Washington University in St. Louis) welcomed us to a Center for Appropriate Technology in the capital, San Salvador, with Central American warmth and caution: "I must warn you: (speaking in perfect English)

"You will get sick from breathing our air."
"You must not drink our water."
"Our food is not healthy and you as visitors will become ill if you eat from our table."
"It is dangerous to preach the gospel here!"

Dr. Navarro was referring to the November 1989 murder of six Jesuit priests, their housekeeper and daughter who sought freedom from violence outside by returning to safety in the university campus. Soldiers trained at the Fort Benning SOA - School of the Americas (Columbus, GA) were responsible for the murders of Jesuits, their housekeeper, daughter and Bishop Oscar Romero.

How can we survive while   breathing *bad air *drinking impure water *eating poor food?

When I heard Navarro's warning about "preaching the gospel as a danger," I felt somewhat justified because during thirty-seven years (1960-1997) in Maryknoll, I perhaps annoyed others for linking the gospel message to care of Earth. I was vilified and /or asked not to speak again in some US churches where the faithful did not want to hear about care of our environment. I remain an "unrepentant offender" in   pairing   Earth care to our spiritual liberation.

Faithful friends and members in St. John's Cathedral of Lafayette, "Oil City", LA informed Monsignor Glenn Provost (now bishop of Lake Charles, LA) of their lack of appreciation over my presence in the cathedral parish. I then chose to leave the church community. With the generous help of our Sierra Club leader, Harold Schoeffler, I moved into one of his inexpensive Lafayette apartments. For human-non-human "community" I bought a Dalmatian puppy and a brown Labrador to keep her company. The dogs welcomed me home after a day of visiting dying hospice patients. It was better to move from St. John's rather than water down my message about Earth care. Parting from St. John's cathedral was bothersome but an amicable separation. My decision to leave was not understood by some members of

---

[30] Quecha word for Mother Earth

the cathedral community. Although surrounded by those who are linked to oil, I do not have personal difficulties with anyone. I simply avoid conflict with family members or friends over the contentious issue of oil.

Lacking enemies[31]
We experience daily
Friendship of our God

Those who challenge all
Fossil fuels are quickly
Considered "unsound"[32]

Blunt showdowns are here
Between defenders of Earth
With those who plunder

---

[31] Some in Lafayette, including a former mayor, despise me for speaking in defense of Earth. However, the venom is in their hearts, not mine. I cannot think of one enemy upon waking, none, when retiring.

[32] A local businessman told me frankly after retiring from the jail, "You will never get another job in this city because you speak for the environment." I have been called a "1960's hippie without the powder" and "New Age pantheist" for holding environmental convictions in Texas and Louisiana. Other unflattering "descriptions" need not be mentioned here. Vulgar, angry messages were quickly deleted from our answering machine to spare Roselyn. Letters of complaint to the local DAILY ADVERTISER are to be expected here.

Chapter 11 - Our Ocean Is Not Too Big To Fail

Dr. Georg Borgstrom, PhD was a Swedish professor of Food Science at Michigan State who privately instructed twenty of us in a 1968 six-week summer seminar on Third World Malnutrition. The classes were held at St. Joseph's University in Philadelphia. Borgstrom was a scholarly, living encyclopedia who wrote a three-volume tome entitled *Fish as Food*. He lectured daily for six weeks without a note, having twenty-five years of teaching experience in Michigan State. His monthly messages regarding the global shortage of food were given on Swedish radio. Georg and Greta Borgstrom became close friends with two invitations to their home in Okemos, near Lansing. As his large book indicated, Borgstrom looked with optimistic confidence to the ocean as a major food source for billions of people. Never did Borgstrom speak of jelly fish as a means of nutrition, even if "jellies" are eaten in some cultures.

Jellies thrive while tuna, cod, Orange Roughy, from New Zealand and other species of fish are declining rapidly. Borgstrom's former dream for the ocean as a source of nutrition is fading away now with the majority of fish species silently vanishing. (Comments from Lisa-ann Gershwin on declining fish stocks are mentioned above)

With fish vanishing
How will seven billion be
Fed in our future

Responsible to several university departments (Geography, Food Science, Economic Geography, and Demography) and a frequent guest lecturer for other deans at Michigan State, Borgstrom, the demographer was quick to remind us human population did not reach one billion until 1800. Thereafter, the growth was frightening in a hungry world.

Rapid population growth led Borgstrom to write *The Hungry Planet*, *Too Many*, along with *Focal Points: A Global Food Strategy, Japan's World Success in Fishing,* plus *World Food Resources.* During lectures Borgstrom became emotional when describing how over fishing and pollution of our ocean were ruining his personal hope of fish providing nutrition for a hungry planet. In the 1960's little was said of ocean acidification from excessive carbon dioxide. Having visited numerous countries as an authority on nutrition, Borgstrom reminded our small class,

"In the 20th century, pure water and toilet paper are luxuries."

Borgstrom in the 1960's ticked off benchmarks of population growth. With the 21st century's declining future of fish, how will nations provide for:

1800 – one billion people
1930 – two billion (doubled in 130 years)
1960 – three billion (doubled in 30 years)
1974 – four billion (doubled in 14 years)
1987 – five billion (doubled in 13 years)
1999 – six billion (doubled in 12 years)

2011 – seven billion (doubled in 12 years)
2044 – eight billion (projection)
2045 – nine billion people (NATIONAL GEOGRAPHIC, January, 2011)

In 2011 as human population reached 7 billion, we might include Borgstrom's reminder from "biological pressure" of several billion more non-human creatures: cattle, pigs, dairy cows, sheep (more sheep in New Zealand than people), and chickens, not to mention pets in affluent societies upon Earth. Borgstrom looked optimistically to the ocean rather than agriculture as a major source of nutrition for *The Hungry Planet*, a title given to one of his books that served as our 1968 Philadelphia seminar text.

Borgstrom that year "erred on the side of conservatism" when he predicted there might be a dozen cities the size of Calcutta by the 21st century. In 2011 there were already twenty-five "megacities" in the world. Earth's top ten population leaders are:

1. Tokyo – 34 million

2. Seoul – 24.4 million

3. Canton (Guangzhou, China) – 24.2 million

4. Mexico City – 23.2 million

5. Delhi – 23.1 million

6. Mumbai (Bombay) – 22.8 million

7. New York City – 22.2 million

8. Sao Paolo, Brazil – 20.9 million

9. Manila – 19.6 million

10. Shanghai – 19.4 million

Jakarta, Indonesia had 900,000 people in 1945. In 2013 the city had over 10 million people in a densely populated area precariously close to the Bay of Jakarta. To where will they flee from the next storm surge? People in Jakarta were going about in boats on January 30, 2014.

We must recall NATIONAL GEOGRAPHIC (January 2011) gave our population growth with a disturbing characteristic: "One out of eleven among seven billion lives in a slum." (Please read *Countdown,* a 2013 book by Alan Weisman regarding population.)

Having lived in Hong Kong during the 1970's when there were a mere four million residents, I recall vividly there were nearly 100,000 people living on small boats, and 30,000 living as "rooftop squatters." If the roof of a building is flat, overcrowded Hong Kong residents who were driven away from illegal shacks in an open space on the ground by the government Squatter Control then "moved higher". Those whose humble huts were demolished by government workers fled to rooftops and felt safe from surprise intrusions by "Yellow Rats" (name given to the HK Squatter Control demolition workers who had to wear yellow hard hats in their dangerous line of wrecking buildings.) It was nearly impossible to gain an accurate census among Hong Kong's millions. Landlords who allowed "rooftop squatters" knew the structures were not legal, but tolerated by the government because of overcrowding in the former British colony.

Hong Kong's population in 2013 was estimated to be 7.2 million in a territory of only 426 square miles. It remains one of the most densely populated regions of the world in 2013. By comparison, Lafayette, LA with over 100,000 people has 47.6 square miles. There are people from outlying areas who dare not drive in Lafayette.

While trying to assist Hong Kong's popular Urban Council member Elsie Elliott-Tu in the 1970's with housing issues and legal matters, it was apparent to twenty-five Chinese volunteers and myself that most families occupied only one room dwellings as roof top shack residents, in shacks on the ground (some legal), on boats, where pets or children might have a rope tied to their legs in case of falling into murky, methane-bubbling waters, crowded in one room public housing units, or in costly private rental apartments. One square foot of real estate in Hong Kong's bustling Central District was estimated to be worth $10,000US in the 1970's. In physics, gravity never takes a vacation. In economics, real estate in commercial zones does not devalue.

A Kowloon, Hong Kong family near Christ the Worker Catholic Church sought relief from overcrowding with sixteen children and adults living in one medium-sized public housing flat. That arrangement totals less than ten square feet per person. Some residents were "illegal" but did not want to be homeless.

Another accommodation was found for the overcrowded family after we invited photographers and reporters from DUNG FONG ("the Eastern area") newspaper to do a photo story in Hong Kong's Chinese daily with over 500,000 readers. Editors put the photo of sixteen living in one room on the front page of their paper. The Hong Kong Housing Authority acted out of embarrassment quickly to relieve such unspeakable population pressure. Journalists would ask for "grist" from Mrs. Elliott and her helpers.

As a school principal over two Muo Kwong (meaning "light") government school institutions and an elected Urban Council member, Mrs. Elliott cleverly advocated frequent use of two major English papers, the SOUTH CHINA MORNING POST and HONG KONG STANDARD, plus some fifty Chinese papers to put pressure upon English-speaking government officials to act. As a British subject, she could not be expelled from Hong Kong, only maligned by officials. Many in government both feared and respected the feisty Elsie Elliott-Tu who was born in 1913. She remains as a revered figure of Hong Kong in 2014 although hobbled by wheel chair mobility. *Avarice, Bureaucracy and Corruption of Hong Kong* (THE ABC's of HONG KONG) is the compelling story of her struggles for justice. Elsie was my mentor for a rewarding decade in Hong Kong.

Economic poverty was common in the British colony but strategically located Social Welfare offices were available for people who needed immediate assistance. Farms in south China and sparse small farms in the New Territories of Hong Kong kept the food supply to millions flowing. The KOWLOON CANTON RAILROAD (KCRR) transported over 5000 pigs daily from China to Hong Kong for slaughter and consumption in a colony where kosher foods were not in high demand.

Chapter 12 - Hong Kong and NOLA Are close To the Ocean's Edge

During the 1970's in Hong Kong, we experienced at least five powerful typhoons. Typhoon Wanda struck Hong Kong, moved west to batter the Portuguese colony of Macau, then turned back to strike Hong Kong a second time. Hong Kong Chinese are survivors. The future for Hong Kong's millions and 300,000 living in New Orleans haunts me. When another Katrina-strength hurricane arrives, escaping NOLA residents might find space for survival when notified in advance of another hurricane.

To where will seven million residents in the former British colony, now under Beijing's control, escape when the South China Sea enters the financial Central District of Hong Kong? There are always more square miles of land to build additional factories producing cheap goods for foreign consumption. However, housing millions of crowded residents will be debated endlessly in a blossoming communist/capitalist system ruled from Beijing planning offices. Economic prosperity has turned China's largest cities into valleys of pollution where children must wear masks to protect their young lungs.

There are over 200 islands near Hong Kong, not all populated. Kai Tak airport was moved from the heart of the Kowloon area to an island in the South China Sea. A third runway is scheduled to be built despite objections of those who wish to protect the shrinking numbers of endangered pink dolphins that inhabit the area.

Japan's Narita airport near Tokyo and the Hong Kong facility (now the 18th largest building in the world) are vulnerable outposts in a world where our ocean is rising. Hong Kong economic planners can hope for continuing growth, with more tourists arriving by plane, but do not care to deal with the matter of a rising ocean level by the next century. Narita airport off Japan and Hong Kong's huge airport are now in the same jeopardized category with vanishing small island nations.

Drowning island nations have formed an Alliance of Small Island States (AOSIS) to plan how to protect their future. Are not continents huge islands surrounded by rising ocean water? We fail to visualize the slowly rising ocean and its acidification.

Chapter 13 - Kiribati Is Not Too Far From Home

We cannot deny
Sea acidification[33]
Warming, rising now

Kiribati is the lowest sea level nation in the world. There are over 100,000 people living on thirty-three islands surrounded by the Pacific. BBC reporters (February 19, 2001) told how this archipelago may eventually be swallowed by a rising Pacific ocean. President Anote Tong has encouraged residents of the threatened islands to leave as rising water continues. In lieu of doubtful mass migration to other Pacific regions, Tong has proposed a multi-billion dollar floating island, something never envisioned before by island dwellers in history.

Benjamin Strauss of Climate Central reports the rising ocean threatens nearly five million US citizens living in communities along coastal areas. They might soon be faced with storm surges that are four feet higher than existing tide levels.

We will not learn much
From the second kick[34] of mules
That we did not know[35]

"Jobs, jobs, jobs" right now
Will assure nobody has
Jobs in the future[36]

Screaming "Jobs, jobs, jobs"
Seldom takes our minds beyond
Five generations[37]

To where will millions
Flee when our rising ocean
Enters their domain?

---

[33] Scientists estimate a 30 percent rise in acidification over the past two centuries

[34] In the first kick of a mule we learned to be on guard (Missouri wisdom)

[35] New York City was completely (stated above) shut down by two "superstorms" Irene (2011) and Sandy (2012) as powerful surges entered the subway tunnels. Who besides Irene and Sandy would close the Stock Exchange?

[36] Economic growth/development based upon unlimited use of fossil fuels will emit more tons of carbon dioxide, exacerbate climate change, leading to global disastrous "weather events" (*Canticle To the Cosmos*, Vol. XII by Brian Swimme)

[37] Native American wisdom postponed decisions until consideration of future generations was discussed thoroughly

There are five oceans – Atlantic, Pacific, Indian, Arctic and Southern. Looking at Earth from space, it appears certain there is only one ocean under different geographic titles. South China and Louisiana have this in common. A warming ocean is expanding and rising. As mentioned before, New Orleans, already twelve feet below sea level, is surviving only by pumps that constantly send water back into the Atlantic or Gulf of Mexico.

The struggle between New Orleans and nature goes back to 1722 when a hurricane devastated the area. In 1794 two hurricanes and a major fire crippled the community. New Orleans weather history is accessible for anyone interested in the vulnerability of an urban area. The US Army Corp of Engineers, federal government and state of Louisiana are presently engaged in ongoing billion dollar efforts to restore wetlands and build coastal barriers for the future.

As legions know in Louisiana gambling casinos, (a cruel taxation upon economic poor people dreaming of getting out of debt) Blackjack is a dealers' game. Nature is the unforgiving dealer in our co-existence. Go beyond the magic twenty-one, we lose in Blackjack. Go beyond 400 parts per million in carbon dioxide emissions, (did so in May 2013) and all beings on Earth will suffer. We continue to environmentally antagonize the invincible power of Earth holding our cards. We continue to deny climate change/global warming. We cannot see how the ocean is succumbing to carbonic acid from greenhouse gases we emit into the atmosphere. We have not all been near the five Islands of plastic that is killing our sacred ocean. Please visit 5 Gyres at 5gyres.org, co-founded by Marcus Eriksen, for their research and communication of the global spread of the five giant gyres. We refuse to think of more "Superstorms" nature will throw at us. Insurance CEO's are very aware of the balance sheets changing.

The great storm of 1938 was the most powerful assault to hit the Atlantic coast before Katrina, Irene and Sandy.

No one wants to hear
Our first state to drown might be
Louisiana[38]

Mike Tidwell is the director of Chesapeake Climate Action Network and author of *Bayou Farewell* who dared to say after Hurricane Katrina: "It is an act of mass homicide to move people back into New Orleans. More hurricanes will follow. The courageous thing to do is to spend money moving people out of New Orleans." Only one time did I see Tidwell's radical suggestion appear in Louisiana newspapers. Moving people out of "The Big Easy," where "Let the good times roll" is the élan, will probably not occur.

---

[38] A US Geological Survey (USGS) map of Louisiana is on the wall of our kitchen in Lafayette. A 700-square mile portion (size of the Washington, D.C.-Baltimore area) of Louisiana will be under water by 2050 as land subsides and our ocean rises. Those who fled from New Orleans as Katrina was arriving on August 29, 2005 might not appreciate suggestions to leave. Nor do residents of precarious rural flood zone area homes wish to spend large sums of money to raise their residence more than ten feet.

On the other side of our world, Hong Kong residents know hours in advance when a typhoon (Chinese word - "big wind") is approaching. Residents can be seen rushing about warning "Daaih Fung, Daaih Fung". This cry in the streets means everyone must get off the streets and find cover. Howling "big winds" will send down flower pots from windows in towering apartments. Next, shacks will be pulverized. Typhoons will rip sheets of tin roofs from shacks and send them like flying guillotine blades into open areas. Such improvised weaponry can decapitate people instantly.

"As human population expands toward 9 billion, the planet's coastlines grow ever more crowded. Fourteen of the seventeen largest cities are built on or very near the edge of the ocean. Half of Earth's population, nearly 3 billion, lives within an hour's drive of a coast." (*Oceans* - The Threats To our Seas and What You Can Do to Turn the Tide by Jon Bowermaster, 2010, p. xii)

Chapter 14 - Alarmists Or Defenders Of Earth?

It was my privilege to consider Georg Borgstrom a friend and mentor for one brief decade. Borgstrom's willingness to express outrage over what we are all doing to harm the ocean and planet placed him very high on a litany of favorite teachers in my life.

Thomas Berry (1914-2009) was the wisest person I ever met. Our friendship began in March 1989 with my simple phone call requesting a visit with Berry someday. "What are you doing for lunch?" was the response from Fr. Berry. That phone call turned out to be a three-hour lunch/seminar in a Yonkers, NY Greek restaurant. Our first encounter was followed by weekly phone chats until Berry's death in June 2009. One week before returning to the cosmos, Thomas said by phone, "I'll be leaving you soon."

Borgstrom with Berry[39]
Having returned home stay as
Constant companions[40]

Are Teilhard, Cousteau, Borgstrom, Berry, Sylvia Earle and contemporary climate scientists, such as James Hansen, "alarmists" or environmental prophets who will not be silent until we begin to see reality through their precocious eyes?

---

[39] Georg Borgstrom, (1913-1990) taught at Michigan State 25 years.
Thomas Berry (1914-2009), founder of the Riverdale Center in New York is a "geologian" a prophetic, wise teacher who was president of the Teilhard Society.

[40] Their teachings remain in my consciousness always.

"There Is Now A Single Issue Before Us: Survival" (Berry)

Vanishing creatures[41]　　　　　　*Are we not aware*
Warn humans "Survival is　　　　　*Of being history's first*
Now our sole issue"[42]　　　　　　*As "terminators"?*

Any half-conscious student of the Cold War knows how we squeaked through Mutual Assured Destruction (MAD) for a half century period unscathed. Which head of state among at least eight nations (five UN Security members –Britain, China, France Russia, USA), plus India, its rival nation Pakistan, Israel (refusing to admit having nuclear weapons) possessing city/nation-destroying weapons, will use nuclear weapons the third time by following the Hiroshima, Nagasaki bombing of August 1945? There are close to 17,000 nuclear weapons in the 21st century. We know Earth can be totally scorched by our nuclear widgets. We woefully lack consciousness of how humans are killing the ocean daily.

How can Earth support[43]　　　　　*"You must not kill" does*
Billions of hungry creatures　　　　*Not yet include Mother Earth*
Without healthy seas?　　　　　　*Who always gives life*
　　　　　　　　　　　　　　　　　　　　　　　　　　　　　MO

THER JONES introduced Sylvia Earle (1935 -   ) to me in the October 2013 issue with a warning: "The following article will make you want to do something about saving the ocean."

Realists like Earle Borgstrom, Berry, Rachel Carson, and Cousteau had already summoned me to leave the sofa for uttering a non-scientific word about our dying ocean.

We cannot deny
Our ocean gives us life which
Is ebbing away

Sylvia Earle, who is called "Her Deepness", was nominated to the Women's Hall of Fame and written up by TIME magazine as "The first hero of the planet."

---

[41] Dr. Peter Raven, retired director of the Missouri Botanical Gardens (St. Louis) reminds us there are more threatened plants than animals. "Nearly 17,000 species are now considered to be threatened with extinction and 869 species are classified as extinct in the wild on International Union for Conservation of Nature's Red List. In the last year (2007) alone 183 species became more endangered. Now in the face of the growing threat posed by environmental changes around the globe, five leading scientists are to argue whether there is a single type of plant or animal which the planet really cannot afford to lose." (COMMON DREAMS NEWS CENTER, November 16, 2008)

[42] Such an awakening call is the jolting , pithy prognosis of Thomas Berry *in Spiritual Ecology: The Cry Of the Earth* , p.17) In one 1982 lecture to a packed auditorium in SMU of Dallas, Berry expressed the same sentiment by summarizing, "We are terminating the Cenozoic Age, going back 70 million years." In a question/discussion session, not one student or faculty member present disputed Berry's warning.

[43] Human population in 2013 was estimated to be 7.122 billion

Earle was preceded by biologist Rachel Carson's discovery of our natural world disappearing rapidly. Publishers nominated *Silent Spring* as one of the most important books of the 20th century. During a lecture given at SMU, Caesar Chavez, the foremost defender of migrant workers was asked if Carson's book could be translated into Spanish for distribution among Spanish-speaking migrant workers. "Ah", said Chavez, to the questioner, that's the book that changed my life."

Sylvia Earle, as a scientist/oceanographer for the National Oceanic and Atmospheric Administration (NOAA) spent the equivalent of 28 days under water around the planet to document decline in the health of our ocean. Earle said with conviction, "97 percent of Earth's water is in the ocean. It is the blue heart of the planet. We should take care of our heart."

Chapter 15 - Elisabeth Kubler-Ross Leaving Our Denial?

While doing research in a US hospital among cancer patients, Dr. Elisabeth Kubler-Ross (1926-2004) noted patients in one particular ward exhibited attitudes that were better than other areas of the facility. Dr. Kubler-Ross discovered a domestic worker with only basic literacy went about her work of cleaning rooms then visited with each patient briefly. After hearing their testimonies of pain and woe, the humble worker, perhaps having endured much suffering in her own personal history calmly replied,

"Honey, it ain't all that bad!"

After a brief word of consolation, she moved on to the next patient. Simple words of comfort from the servant who took time from cleaning to console women and men in pain helped to raise the psychological wellbeing of all patients in the ward

Dr. Kubler-Ross looked upon death as the "final stage of growth."(Please read *The Stages of Death and Dying* by Dr. Kubler-Ross)

From 1995 until 1998 as chaplain for Hospice of Acadiana, I met with over 3000 dying patients in the Lafayette, LA area. I tried my best to implement Dr. Kubler-Ross' teaching and help hospice patients overcome denial, anger, depression then peacefully accept the inevitability of death. I wished the best to those bargaining patients who chose to leave their homes or hospital beds then spend time and money by going to M.D. Anderson in Houston for a brief extension of their hurting lives.

As patients receive a message of finality from her/his doctor about a lingering illness and are told of its terminal nature, there are phases of "growth" that must soon be endured:

*DENIAL – When told test results are returned that indicate only so much time remains in life, our initial reaction might be to charge the medical messenger with making a mistake.

*ANGER – Doctors, nurses or family members who announce to someone their serious illness will soon lead to death could themselves become the target of an emotional, angry outburst from the medicated, suffering patient. When asked to sign medical papers while in the moment of receiving indications of life about to end, patients have been known to throw pens at the wall or exhibit hostility directly at the person who brought news of impending death.

*BARGAINING – If news of death is presented to young patients, they may instinctively begin to bargain for an extension of time. Elderly patients resist death till the end on occasion.

If patients were suffering intensely, they might even beg for an early death to free them from unspeakable agony. Hospice doctors and nurses are skilled "pain managers." Morphine has limitations in relief from pain. During three years as a hospice chaplain I did not encounter any patients who courted suicide.

*DEPRESSION – These phases of passage/growth need not be like clockwork. Throughout the entire process, there is genuine sadness or depression. The phases/stages may be freely, flexibly interwoven during final days of life.

*PEACEFUL ACCEPTANCE – At some liberating moment, the patient might break through denial, bargaining, sadness and admit with wise Native Americans, "Life is brief as the breath of a buffalo in winter" or "Any day is a good day for dying." Having attained the final acceptance stage, a deep sense of freedom may be realized.

Some liberated young patients admit to themselves, "It is no disgrace to die at an early age." One patient in Hong Kong openly accepted death in his 30's.

Dr. Kubler-Ross had spoken to thousands and her writings were translated into many languages. Did she ever relate the phases of growth to care of Earth? That association was not likely her intention. However, there is an ecological parallel to be examined in our era when the Earth is in peril and humans are the major threat to a tolerable future.

*DENIAL – Although 97 percent of climate scientists agree global warming/climate change are realities brought on by humankind, by the end of January 2014, 23 percent of US citizens do not believe in global warming. At the same time 29 members of the US Congress do not believe there is global warming. Some PhD's, according to my personal experience, are known to be in denial of climate change. The Koch Brothers and fossil fuel supporters continue to quote (and pay) some academics as their "scientific support" for denial of climate change.

*ANGER – Those who refuse to accept scientific information about climate change express anger and engage in emotional outbursts when the subject surfaces. Likewise, scientists and proponents of Earth's warming express anger and frustration with those who refuse to believe obvious changes in climate. A biased but calm opinion is offered in *The Age of Stupid*

*BARGAINING – Parents of young children express a desire for their children's future to be free from violent storms or hurricanes. NASA scientist James Hansen wrote *Storms of My Grandchildren* to reduce threats of climate events for them. People in their 80's or beyond become environmental "activists" to protect the future of coming generations. Hansen knows the storms expected for his grandchildren are already wreaking havoc in the present. He has been arrested for protests against the Keystone XL pipeline bringing tar sands oil from Canada to Texas. Hansen's "civil disobedience" is obedience to a scientific consciousness. Bill McKibben and thousands of supporters formed www.350.org as a global "bargaining force" for reducing carbon emissions below 350 parts per million.

*DEPRESSION – We will feel deep sadness over the barren demise of US prairies, tree losses, disappearance of sixty million buffalo, millions of prairie chickens and the last passenger pigeon, "Martha" dying in 1914 in a Cincinnati zoo. In the 21st century there might be a total of only 100 Florida panthers. Eastern cougars were declared extinct on March 2, 2011. Caregivers in the province of Szechwan, China are struggling to keep less than 1000 surviving pandas alive and well. Pandas exist in the wild only in that remote province of China which means "four rivers."

Can we imagine
Life without the black-white face
Of sacred pandas

Passenger pigeons[44]
Flew overhead in millions
Seen now on You Tube

When animals leave
Part of humankind expires
Not to be revived

---

[44] Migrating clouds of pigeons might take days to go by. Our ancestors killed them off.

Chapter 16 - Our Oppression Of Earth Must Die

The most important growth phase for humans is acceptance of death. In planetary thinking humans will reach a stage of honest realization that our destructive way of life must die – if we are to survive.

PEACEFUL ACCEPTANCE – Humans who evolve from our reptilian, mammal brains toward Teilhard's state of higher consciousness might finally admit; our profligate fossil fuel burning style of life should cease, if others are to live in the future. Would Elisabeth Kubler-Ross forgive anyone for attaching her phases of growth to preservation of Earth's threatened environment? A growing chorus of "green" people speaks for Earth, yet overlooks an ocean in dire straits because of carbon dioxide.

We must stop killing
Earth's vast ocean through belching
Carbon dioxide

"We cannot live here
Anymore"[45] might someday be
Said of our planet

---

[45] Residents near areas of "fracking" interviewed in Gasland 2 by Josh Fox

Chapter 17 - Our Renewable Energy Revolution

For four decades Amory Lovins and members of the Rocky Mountain Institute have been promoting a weaning of society away from fossil fuels and encouraging our global transition to renewable energy sources. Such forward thinking is certainly not new.

During a 1931 conversation with Henry Ford and Harvey Firestone, Thomas Alva Edison (1847-1931) is reported to have said, "We should turn to the inexhaustible energy supplies of nature: solar, wind, and tides. I'd put my money on solar."

 In just one moment, Sun emits more energy than all other known sources of energy throughout our 10,000 year history. But the limitless sources of energy cannot be marketed. Therefore powerful corporate entities will promote "Flat Earth denial" of environmental problems, bollix any proposal to utilize renewable energies and maintain imprisonment of Earth in a carbon-based system that is harmful to life.

Precisely because of money, the managers of fossil fuel corporations will retain a key that keeps Earth locked into the imaginary planetary cell block by burning fossil fuels.

Will we run out of oil
In time to save ourselves
From great disasters?

"Fracking" has been mentioned above. Its threat merits repetition. Residents of areas where hydraulic fracturing is contaminating their air, water and soil were interviewed by Josh Fox in *Gasland 2*. Some said, "We cannot live here anymore."

97% of climate scientists agree that continued burning of fossil fuels will make survival very difficult for all on Earth.

Chapter 18 - We May Be Winning Support Without Knowing How Much

Mark Hertsgaard is author of *Hot: Living through the Next Fifty Years*

Optimistically he points out "We're actually wining the fight against climate change, but most people don't know it yet. That may be a strange statement to make in a week when a landmark scientific report declares that humanity must quit fossil fuels within thirty years or risk catastrophic climate change.

"The Intergovernmental Panel on Climate Change (IPCC) Report on September 27, effectively endorsed activist Bill McKibben's argument that most of the Earth's remaining fossil fuels must stay in the ground. The IPCC calculated from this day forward, humanity can burn no more than one-half of 1 trillion metric tons of carbon if we are to have a better than 50-50 chance of limiting global temperature rise to 2 degrees Celsius above pre-industrial levels. At current rates, this 'carbon budget' will be used up by the early 2040's. The upshot: the great bulk of the 3 trillion tons of fossil fuels still underground must remain there." (*Behold the Rising Sun*, THE NATION, October 21, 2013)

Ironically, THE NATION cover story is about luxury real estate being bought and sold for millions of dollars per unit. Former exiled dictators and underworld figures are major players in the real estate market of Florida. Little consideration is given to the future when Florida will possibly be the first state to fall victim as the warming, rising Atlantic overwhelms it.

Urban planners are somewhat mindful of threats from unlimited burning coal and oil. Therefore natural gas has been put forth as an environmental "savior" that generates less carbon dioxide.
Several city busses running on natural gas in "Oil City" bear the art work: "POWERED BY NATURE" as they pass by; transporting very few passengers in car-loving Lafayette.

Louisiana Gulf Coast Oil Exposition (LAGCOE) takes turns with Odessa, Texas in hosting a conference on energy extracted from the Gulf of Mexico. 2013 was Lafayette's turn to host LAGCOE as Odessa, Texas sat out this year. Restaurants and hotels in Lafayette were bustling as 17,000 delegates came to "Oil City" from 47 states and 43 nations. Earlier in the month there was a job fair held in Lafayette. THE DAILY ADVERTISER (October 24, 2013) headline doubtless, brought cheers to those who meet in the Lafayette Petroleum Club:

"PLANT COULD BE BOON FOR ENERGY"

With no more futuristic anxiety than Florida real estate brokers about a rising ocean, "Jason French of Cheniere Energy seemed to be swept up in his message that the $12 billion Sabine Pass natural gas export facility will be a jobs-and-energy jackpot for Louisiana. A single tank of natural gas inside the facility could power the entire state of Louisiana for a day; 21/2 tanks could power all of Texas in one day, French said, pointing to a diagram that showed five tanks. By 2015, we'll be producing more than we can use. Total construction should be done in 2019." (Front page article) Surely, there were some among the standing-only crowd listening to Mr. French who recalled Hurricane Audrey that devastated the Gulf coast in 1957, followed by Alex and Rita in 2005.

A Lafayette nurse and budding photographer gave me his video copy of Cameron, LA, where a 49-bed Memorial hospital was thoroughly demolished in 2005 by Hurricane Rita. Having visited the Hiroshima Museum in 1982, I quickly made mental comparisons between scenes in barren, devastated Cameron, LA and Hiroshima following the bombing in 1945.

There is no radioactivity in Cameron or other Gulf coast communities that were flattened by nature's fury. Any plans for expansion of energy facilities in the Gulf region are through the courtesy of Mother Earth. If hurricanes could destroy buildings, including a sturdy hospital in Cameron, what might happen to Liquified Natural Gas (LNG) operations on the Gulf coast? When hurricanes are picked up coming across the Atlantic, PHI helicopters are at the ready to remove thousands of workers before storms enter the Gulf.

Regardless of the momentarily calm Gulf weather, natural gas is always generating carbon dioxide. Any fossil fuel feeds the unprecedented weather changes Earth is undergoing in our challenging times.

Scientists and national leaders are not dreaming when proposing carbon neutrality.

Chapter 19 - Four Nations Racing For Carbon Neutrality

Iceland, Norway, New Zealand and Costa Rica are striving to be first among 195 nations to be described as "carbon neutral." Although Norway is one of the foremost oil producing nations, leaders must perceive carbon dioxide emissions are a global threat that can be countered with our need to promote the carbon neutrality revolution.

Pope Benedict XVI called for installation of solar panels on all buildings of Vatican City, a tiny enclave of only 109 acres within the heart of Rome. Nevertheless, the "Green Pope" will be recognized for support of carbon neutrality.

Benedict is in ecological sync with Mohammed Nasheed, president of the Maldives. The island nation is surrounded by a rising ocean. Nasheed comments on carbon neutrality, "In that regard, I would invite everyone living in a country that has not signed up to carbon neutrality to ask their elected representatives why they are dragging their feet on the most important issue in human history." (*Climate Change and the Ocean*, an interview with Mohamed Nasheed, the Maldives, *Oceans*, p. 66)

Stanford University and Cornell are just two of several institutions working in unison on the urgent issue of leaving fossil fuels in the ground as we transition to renewable energy sources. Moving away from addiction to fossil fuels to carbon neutrality is the most important global occurrence in our Anthropocene age.

What are forty years[46]
When compared to billions in
Renewable sources?

---

[46] Hydraulic fracturing is a desperate effort to squeeze more than forty years of oil from Earth.

Chapter 20 - Apartheid Was Brought Down By Divestment

www.greencentury.com and **www.gofossilfree.org** are non-violent methods of wresting economic power and control from powerful fossil fuel corporations by simply encouraging divestment in such multinationals.

"Since winter of 2012, more than 300 campaigns have sprouted on college campuses calling for their respective schools to divest endowment funds from the fossil fuel industry (NATIONAL CATHOLIC REPORTER, November 8, 2013). Students who are anxious about their future in a warming world are encouraging universities in the US now to transfer their endowments toward corporations that support renewable energies.

The powerful apartheid apparatus of South Africa was debilitated by gradual economic divestment in an unjust system. Subjecting Earth to limitless burning of fossil fuels is a global injustice that screams for transformation.

Chapter 21 - Solar Powered Planes?

In 1903 Wilbur Wright predicted "heavier than air flight will not be possible for another fifty years."

Michael Caruso, editor of THE SMITHSONIAN wrote: "In 1960 people around the world made 25 million trips outside their home countries. In 2012 that number passed one billion." (From *The Editor*, April 2013)

Carbon tax on flights is very controversial. The European Union (EU) and United Nations are supportive of a carbon tax on plane travel. President Obama rejected such a plan. China is opposed to the tax on plane tickets. Air plane voyagers grumble over extra fees for baggage. How do we reduce carbon dioxide lacing Earth from huge luxurious jetliners?

The "iconic Boeing 747 airliner is fading into the horizon" (Associated Press, October 25, 2013). Why place four powerful engines on a plane when two are sufficient?

On a flight from Hong Kong to the USA in 1982, a fire broke out in the number four engine of our 747, forcing us to land in Frankfurt, Germany. Extinguishers inside the engine put out the small fire and we landed safely at 8:30AM. Not until 8:30PM did we get help from Sir Freddie Laker's now defunct Peoples' Airline. Laker sent an antiquated Electra turbo-prop plane to pick up stranded passengers and move us on to London. He was present at the gate in Heathrow to personally greet each one of us after midnight.

A solar powered plane, the size of a 747 flew from San Francisco to NYC on May 28, 2010. The solar powered plane stored enough energy to fly at night. If corporations consent to the radical transition in powering airplanes, it will occur. Transition from fossil fuels to renewable resources depends upon our awakening. Novelist Bernard Malamud said, "Conscience and conscience alone will turn the world upside down."

We must change our lives
More in coming decades than the
Past ten thousand years

Chapter 22 - Each Building Might Be Powered By Renewables

UNIVAC computers from the 1950's occupied a city block. In 2013 sophisticated "smart phones" contain the digital capacity of antiquated 1950's computers. They do not require a city block. Children now carry such computers in their pockets.

Is literature[47]
Our reflection of Earth's
Consciousness or words?

Publishers chose *Silent Spring* as the most important book of the past fifty years. Carson's book presented a "state of the Earth" for all to consider.

Could Lisa-ann Gershwin's book on jellyfish be a 21st century documentation regarding the "state of the ocean" for all to ponder?

We cannot deny
Sea acidification
Warming, rising now

---

[47] Historian Arthur Schlesinger selected Shakespeare (1564-1616) as the most influential person of the millennium

Chapter 23 - Giants Can Be Brought Down Without Violence

The biblical David as pessimist remarked upon seeing Goliath: "How can I win?" David the optimist countered: "How can I miss?"

"We the people versus" I

The Department of Defense (DOD) during the Cold War surrounded Kansas City, MO with 150 Minuteman II nuclear missiles. A small group of Missouri Peace Planters decided that the missiles should be removed and the prairie land returned to agriculture. There were nearly 1000 missiles spread throughout Midwestern states. However, a small determined local group of KCMO peacemakers continued vigils at nearby sites. Eventually, the DOD removed all the missiles. Obsolescence of such weapons is a factor, but non-violent pressure from citizens, like water dripping on stone, eventually makes a path. The 150 missiles once ("imprisoning") KCMO were still missing in January 2014 after speaking to Jane and Henry Stoever ,two of the original "Peace Planters" in Kansas City.

Missiles may be absent from farm land. However, Washington wants to remain the sole superpower through military might. The US Air Force B-2 bomber is now based in Whiteman AFB near Knob Noster, MO. The 509th Bomb wing is a joint Army, Navy, Air Force base. The B-2 can fly to Asia, pass over all of Afghanistan in just 45 minutes at 900 mph, and wreak tremendous carpet bombing damage, then return to Missouri for cocktails and an evening meal. Drones are also launched and controlled from Whiteman AFB, where agriculture was once dominant. After a decade of fruitless warfare and billions of dollars spent on devastation, the US is withdrawing from Afghanistan and the longest war in our history. To where will B-2 bombers be sent next?

"We the people versus" II

In the 1980's the Department of Energy (DOE) informed residents of Waxahachie (means "Buffalo chips" in a Native American language) fifteen minutes east of Dallas that a multi-billion dollar Superconducting Supercollider (SSC) would be built beneath their rural homes. This DOE announcement was not warmly received by Waxahachie citizens. They held meetings in churches, restaurants and confronted a large gathering of scientists who were invited by DOE officials to tour Texas.

One dairy farmer was ordered to seal his water wells because the DOE knew radioactivity would seep into wells and cows would be producing radioactive milk. In a peaceful confrontation with scientists invited by the DOE, residents demanded to know how radioactivity could be kept from their environment. Scientists denied awareness of radioactivity in the process.

A large elliptic tunnel was dug at great expense beneath Waxahachie, then suddenly funding ceased for the SSC collider. Perhaps the dark tunnel could be used for raising mushrooms, as it is all that remains of a project that might have hired several hundred scientists. Fire ants quickly ate away at the failed DOE tar baby. Texans knew colliders already existed in the Fermi National Laboratory near

Batavia, Illinois and another collider in Switzerland. Waxahachie residents rejoiced when the SSC Goliath fell back into non-being.

A few Missouri Peace Planter "David's" and handful of Waxahachie residents represent a growing number of little people who take on (and defeat) giant monsters bent on exploiting Earth.

The National Resources Defense Council (NRDC) lists dozens of grass root environmental groups that exist in our neighborhoods.

Anyone who is in favor of clean air, pure water, healthy food is an ecologist. More are turning off inane television programs, rising from their sofas and challenging power brokers who do not care about future generations.

Chapter 24 - What Do Theologians Say About Our Ecological Future?

"Heaven as God's throne and Earth as God's footstool" (Matthew 5:35), cited above is clearly a foundational expression of spiritual ecology.

Franciscans are followers of St. Francis of Assisi (1182-1226) who is considered the patron saint of ecologists. Fr. Richard Rohr (1943 -) is a member of the Franciscans who contributed a mind-expanding essay *"Creation as the Body of God"* in a collection entitled *Spiritual Ecology*. Rohr quotes Thomas Aquinas (1225-1274) who said, "Creation is the primary and most perfect revelation of the Divine."

Rohr cites another Franciscan theologian/philosopher John Duns Scotus (1265-1308) who observed "God remains in immediate sustaining attentiveness to everything that exists, precisely in its 'thisness'"

Philosophy ("love of wisdom") and Theology ("Study about God and religion") were two subjects I pursued from 1960 until 1967 while in Maryknoll seminaries. I searched periodicals and text books for deeper understanding about rejection of war as a means of diplomacy (The Kellogg-Briand pact 1928). Despite biblical mandates "You must not kill", the irrelevant "Just War" theory was a 1960's topic being debated in our world with "Weapons of Mass Destruction" (WMD's).

The 1982 US bishops' pastoral letter "Challenge of Peace" was the most relevant document on the immorality of deterrence and nuclear war. The bishops had enough courage to challenge "deterrence" (Latin root is "to terrorize") but did not specifically denounce nuclear war. The United Nations had already condemned use of nuclear weapons as a crime in 1962. The UN preceded some Vatican II documents (*The Church in the Modern World*) that had gone further in denouncing "city-destroying weapons." (Paragraph 82). Little is told of Christians in the first 300 years who refused military involvement of any nature. Presently, some major Christian Universities host Reserved Officer Training Corps (ROTC) for all branches of the military. From 1955-1957, I was forced to endure Army ROTC training in the University of Dayton, a Catholic institution.

"Ecology" however was not even a working term during the 1960's. When visiting a Presbyterian church in Vera Dero, Cuba in 1986, I came upon a book entitled *Theoecologia*. (Theological ecology). From reading Latin American theology in the 1980's I discovered a vital connection between theology and ecology. "*Theoecologia*" appeared as "oecologia" in 2014 on the Internet even though I had seen the term nearly thirty years earlier.

Again, I looked in retrospect to Thomas Berry, a follower of Teilhard for connecting theology and ecology. Berry taught, "Ecology is the basis of every subject."

Not until 2013 did Richard Rohr open my eyes to reflect on two "incarnations." The first is an unmentioned cosmic occurrence billions of years ago; the second a human/Divine Incarnation we remember in global celebrations on December 25th.

Father Rohr reminds us, "The Incarnation of God did not happen in Bethlehem two thousand years ago. That is just when some of us started taking it seriously. The incarnation actually happened approximately 14.5 billion years ago with a moment we now call the 'Big Bang.' That is when God actually decided to materialize and to expose who God is." (*Spiritual Ecology*, p. 236)

There are some who refer to the first incarnation more maternally, gently as the "Big Birth." Without the cosmic birth of Earth billions of years ago, there could not be a personal intervention of Christ as Compassion personified in human history. Colossal threats to the first cosmic incarnation exist from our environmental and militaristic activities gone amok.

Grover Foley, PhD received his degree in theology at Basle, Switzerland under Karl Barth, one of the foremost theologians in modern history. Forty years ago Foley wrote "*Reaping the Whirlwind: The Question of Faith in an Obsolete World.*" (CROSS CURRENTS Vol. XXIII, Fall 1973)

Foley reflects on mind-numbing environmental and military challenges of our age. He quotes Einstein who said, "The unleashed power of the atom changed everything except our way of thinking, and thus we drift toward unparalleled catastrophe." (*Will Man (sic) Become Extinct?"* War/Peace Report, January 1967, p. 9)

Foley observes that the one (such as Einstein) who warns of madness is in danger of being judged as mad. "This involves a risk, for in the eyes of a mad world the one who warns, will herself/himself appear mad." (Foley, CROSS CURRENTS, p. 295)

Aware of unprecedented environmental and military challenges confronting us in the present, Foley poses this scenario: "In the face of disaster it is not important whether we will or will not change the world in time. In fact, we almost certainly WILL NOT." (Emphasis is Foley's)

"What is important is that we change ourselves, do the right thing, and give them warning." (Please read Ezekiel 3:17)

Change ourselves often　　　　　　　　　*Never stop growing*
Giving gentle warnings to　　　　　　　*In kindness toward Earth since*
Those who are dozing　　　　　　　　　*There are no limits*

"God is Love"[48] pouring　　　　　　　*Military in*
Forth in gifts of nature far　　　　　　　*Our age may mean protection*
Beyond adjectives　　　　　　　　　　　*From angry nature[49]*

Bolivian President Evo Morales (1959 -   ) spoke with wisdom for all elected officials and religious leaders: "We should immediately stop spending money on warfare and devote all our resources to defending nations against global warming."

---

[48] I John 4:16

[49] February 22, 2004 the Pentagon issued a warning to President Bush that global warming was a greater threat than terrorism. The warning was kept secret, but THE OBSERVER (UK) obtained a copy.

Thomas Merton wrote "The Ecological Conscience" in 1968. He urged that we all "Develop an ecological conscience – and fast." An ocean overwhelmed by carbon dioxide and plastic reminds us not to delay changing our lives. Jellyfish will survive in carbonic plasticity while we cannot.

**There is no stronger
Teacher in history than
Our sacred ocean**

Index